INSIDE THE MIND OF
THE GOLDEN STATE KILLER

Other titles in the *Inside the Mind* series

INSIDE THE MIND OF
THE
GOLDEN
STATE
KILLER

JOSEPH JAMES DEANGELO JR

BRAD HUNTER

G:

Published in 2025
by Gemini Gift Books
Part of Gemini Books Group

Based in Woodbridge and London

Marine House, Tide Mill Way,
Woodbridge, Suffolk IP12 1AP
United Kingdom

www.geminibooks.com

Text and design © 2025 Gemini Gift Books Ltd

ISBN 978-1-80247-338-4

Disclaimer

The information presented in this book is based on extensive research of publicly
available materials and other published media reports. The publisher and authors
have made every effort to ensure the accuracy and completeness of the information
at the time of publication. However, as media reports can sometimes contain
inaccuracies or be subject to change over time, the author and publisher cannot
guarantee the absolute accuracy of every detail presented. Furthermore, every
reasonable effort has been made to trace the copyright-holders of any material
reproduced in this book, but if any have been inadvertently overlooked, the publisher
would be glad to hear from them.

This book may contain graphic descriptions of violence and other disturbing content
that may be upsetting to some readers. Reader discretion is advised.

Manufacturer's EU Representative: Eurolink Compliance Limited, 25 Herbert Place,
Dublin, D02 AY86, Republic of Ireland. admin@eurolink-europe.ie

Printed in the UK

10 9 8 7 6 5 4 3 2

Contents

Introduction

Soon-to-be-retired homicide detective Paul Holes parked outside the tidy family bungalow on Canyon Oak Drive.

He sat behind the wheel, studying the house itself, the vehicle in the driveway, the neighbourhood. What kind of person lived there? What was he like?

Was he the homicidal maniac that cops suspected?

Was he the long-elusive Golden State Killer?

Investigators knew that the elderly man living in the home shared it with his daughter and granddaughter. There wasn't much else.

That was 23 April 2018.

On that day in Citrus Heights, California, a suburb of the state capital Sacramento, the weather was a balmy 84°F (29°C), and there wasn't a cloud in the sky. However, dark clouds of a different kind were gathering over the quiet enclave.

What the elderly man inside the tidy home didn't know was that detectives were about to drop a bombshell at his doorstep. Investigators suspected that the man inside was a serial killer and sadistic rapist.

"Well, after 24 years of pursuing this Golden State Killer, utilizing new technology, this genetic genealogy technology, about a week prior, I had been made aware that this Joseph DeAngelo was possibly related to the Golden State Killer," retired cold-case detective Paul Holes told NPR in 2019.

"And after investigating him for a week, and realizing I was going to be retiring the following week, I decided he was a prime suspect. And every time I had a prime suspect in this case, I have to go see, where are they living? What are they driving? What is the neighbourhood they're living in like?"

A day before the killer was arrested, ending four decades of terror, Holes made his trek to the murderer's lair and parked in front.

"His car was in the driveway. I knew he was home. But I've been here with prime suspects before. Was he *really* the guy? And so I started debating, well, I'm retiring tomorrow – or actually just turning my badge and gun in the next day," the veteran investigator said.

"I'm not sure he really is the Golden State Killer. So I started to debate. Should I just go knock on this guy's door? He's a former law enforcement officer. Maybe I can establish a bond saying, 'Hey, you're a former cop, and you understand how this goes. I'm looking into an old case,' you know, chuckle, chuckle. And, you know, 'Let's just get this over with. Give me a sample of DNA, and you'll never be contacted by an investigator on this case again if you're not the guy.'"

Something stopped Holes dead in his tracks.

"But as I sat there, I realized the various aspects that led him to become a prime suspect I could not dismiss. And I didn't want to blow the case, the case that was my passion for a quarter century at that point. And I decided I probably should let things lie. And I drove off," he said.

Throughout his long career in law enforcement, Holes admitted he was mostly a lone wolf, and that was why he decided to take a peek at his quarry before a media circus blasted the story across the nation's front pages and airwaves.

"And, you know, in hindsight, this was foolish from an officer safety standpoint because if I had gone up and knocked on his door, if he recognized me or decided he did not want to be caught, things could have gone very bad for me," Holes said, adding that his quarry was known to be proficient with a gun.

A doorknock could have gone south and torpedoed Holes's retirement before it even began. There was no backup. Just Holes and the man detectives had zeroed in on as the notorious Golden State Killer.

The chilling moniker had been coined by the late crime writer Michelle McNamara, who became obsessed with the investigation and whose reporting put the murderer on the map. He had previously been an amalgam of three separate predators: the Visalia Ransacker, the East Area Rapist and the Original Night Stalker.

Around 2 p.m. on 24 April 2018, neighbours said they spotted Joseph James DeAngelo Jr, 72, tinkering in his garage with a table he was building and fiddling around his beloved front lawn. These were the final pedestrian chores of a middle-class life that was about to be turned upside down.

At about 4 p.m., cops swooped in.

DeAngelo was arrested and initially charged with eight counts of first-degree murder, based on DNA evidence. More charges lurked on the horizon.

He had a roast in the oven when the cops arrived, and he asked them if he could turn off the heat. His daughter and granddaughter were out at the time, something the investigators had planned on.

Investigators later said that the suspected killer had been under surveillance for several days as cops tuned into his habits. They waited until he was outside the house before springing into action.

They retrieved a Suzuki motorcycle, a fishing boat and two newer model cars – a Volvo and a Toyota. DeAngelo would not need them anymore.

The lightning arrest, conducted by a Special Weapons and Tactics (SWAT) team supplemented by federal and local police officers, stunned the suspected killer's neat Citrus Heights neighbourhood. Around 30 federal, state and local law enforcement personnel then began coming through the modest house with the neatly trimmed lawn. The task force also included investigators from Southern California who had a lot of skin in the game. DeAngelo's home was just several miles away from the scene of a slew of brutal rapes that terrorized eastern Sacramento County during the 1970s.

Cops later revealed that the suspected Golden State Killer had been identified through something called forensic genetic genealogy. It was a pioneering moment in the annals of crime detection and has helped clear hundreds of cold cases in the intervening years.

But just who was Joseph James DeAngelo Jr? In many ways, he remains a mystery to this day, even to those who thought they knew him.

Around the middle-class Citrus Heights neighbourhood where he lived, reviews were mixed on DeAngelo's personality. He was known around the area as "Joe" – a somewhat cantankerous, odd man with a booming voice and an obsession with his front lawn.

DeAngelo, some neighbours said, had a bad temper, with one saying the portly senior vowed to "deliver a load of death" over a barking dog. Others told the *Sacramento Bee* that he would randomly scream obscenities if one of his innumerable chores went off the rails.

The verdict was that Joseph James DeAngelo was an angry, troubled individual. And it was best to avoid him.

Records revealed that he had lived in the house since at least 1983 and that he was divorced. He lived with his daughter and granddaughter in a ranch-style home. Another daughter was a successful emergency room surgeon.

"It's terrifying to think this man could have hopped the fence and come into my backyard. I have children," Beth Walsh told the *Sacramento Bee*, adding that she lived behind DeAngelo on an adjacent street. "I'm glad to know they caught this guy."

Other neighbours went on to describe his countless meltdowns. Big things, little things. It didn't seem to matter. But the message for folks in Citrus Heights seemed to be: Stay out of my face.

"We used to just call him 'Freak'," Natalia Bedes-Correnti, who lived a few houses away, told the *Bee*. "He used to have these temper tantrums, not at anybody, just [expressing] his self-frustration … usually because he couldn't find his keys."

The "Freak" was so loud that neighbours could hear his verbal explosions inside their homes. However, they added that the tantrums had suddenly stopped several years prior.

Eddie Verdon said his one encounter with the retired man sent chills down his spine. He caught DeAngelo prowling on his property. "I had the creeps about this guy for a long time," he said.

Another neighbour, Grant Gorman, grew up in the house behind DeAngelo's. Gorman said his neighbour was so angry and frightening that he avoided playing with the killer's daughter when they were children.

"I felt sorry for her," he said. "This guy just had this anger that was just pouring out of him. He'd just be yelling at nothing in the backyard, pacing in circles."

Gorman added that in 1994, DeAngelo took umbrage at his family's Rottweiler. It came in the form of a phone call, and the Gormans were certain it was Joe DeAngelo. If the family didn't stop their dog from barking, the caller vowed that "he was going to deliver a load of death".

On another occasion, he came into the family's backyard demanding that Gorman's mother, Sonja, stop mowing her lawn. It was bothering him, which neighbours found ironic given his own obsessive devotion to home and garden maintenance.

Not taking any chances, the Gorman family installed a lock on their back gate just in case the situation ever escalated.

"He was the kind of person you didn't want to make mad," said Sonja Gorman. "There were enough times where we just knew not to bother him and not to incite him."

But DeAngelo was also the kind of man who could be neighbourly and pass the time of day, chirping over the fence on a Saturday afternoon.

Cory Harvey told reporters that "Joe" had told her that he had retired two weeks previously. It was something he had looked forward to, and he said he intended to do a lot of fishing and biking. He would start enjoying the good life, he said.

Harvey lived next to DeAngelo for eight years and said he was a good neighbour, even helping to pay for a fence between their two homes. He was, she said, a regular guy.

"Except for that quirkiness of getting mad," she said, adding that when DeAngelo realized she was within hearing distance, he would shout an apology.

Gabby Ramirez, 14, was a close friend of the crusty old man's granddaughter. She said the suspect was pleasant.

"From what I can remember, he was just a normal grandpa," Ramirez said. "He would take us out to go and get something to eat. He was nice to us."

But the prevailing view of the grumpy grandfather was a negative one. And that extended beyond his neighbourhood.

For many years, he was a regular at a joint called Charlie's Café in Citrus Heights.

Owner Charlene Carte told *People* that DeAngelo would shuffle into his favourite booth usually twice a week. Once seated, he would bark orders at the servers. This would typically be followed by complaints about his food. Carte and her staffers called the man "Mr Happy" for his sour demeanour. She was stunned when she discovered DeAngelo's alter ego was the Golden State Killer.

"I was in shock," she said. "It's scary to know I was that close [to him]."

The diner is typically packed, ironically often with law enforcement personnel, and offers country-style home cooking. DeAngelo would typically order breakfast or lunch, with tuna salad being a particular favourite.

"This guy has been on the run for 40 years," Carte said. "This is scary, knowing I've talked to this man, had many conversations with him, dealt with his attitude and anger. And any time, he could've snapped."

She added, "He never showed any signs that he was on the run. He never showed any signs that he was a killer or a rapist. He was just your Average Joe, but a grumpy old man."

Joseph James DeAngelo Jr was a long way from merely being an oldster screaming at kids to keep off his grass, cops revealed.

During a horrific stretch – 1976 to 1986 – the Golden State Killer has been linked by DNA and modus operandi to 13 murders, 51 rapes and more than 120 burglaries from Sacramento to Southern California's Orange County.

His victims ranged in age from 13 to 41 and included women at home alone or with their children or husbands. The sickening attacks began in Sacramento with the 18 June 1976 rape of a woman in the Rancho Cordova–Carmichael area.

Detectives believe his final crime was a 1986 murder.

But for decades, DeAngelo slipped between the cracks and was able to lead a semblance of a normal life even while he prowled the night hunting for potential victims. Only genetic genealogy would shatter his quiet – if angry – life. For generations of detectives, Joseph James DeAngelo Jr was never on their radar until the perverse play's final act.

And when the curtains were pulled back, a sadistic monster was revealed. One of the most violent and feared criminals in Californian history had been brought to justice.

As the thin gruel of details emerged about his life in the days after his arrest, there were several remarkable features on DeAngelo's CV.

For starters, he was a former cop who earned a criminal justice degree from Sacramento State University following two tours of duty in the US Navy during the Vietnam War, where he was decorated for valour.

Investigators believed that while he was a police officer in the Sacramento area, DeAngelo committed countless burglaries, rapes and murders. His law enforcement career crashed and burned when he was nabbed stealing a hammer and dog repellent from a Citrus Heights drug store. Both items are handy tools for the enterprising burglar – or rapist.

DeAngelo was even once part of a 100-officer task force hunting the so-called Visalia Ransacker, who burglarized homes, leaving them a defiled disaster zone. It would later be revealed that it was DeAngelo who was, in fact, the Visalia Ransacker.

Survivors described their tormentor as deft and "unusually cruel", who raped scores of women during his violent odyssey. There were the taunts, the humiliation, the terror and, for most of his victims, the never-ending nightmares.

Upon graduation from police college, according to the local *Exeter Sun*, DeAngelo believed that "without law and order there can be no government and without a democratic government, there can be no freedom. Law enforcement is his career, he says, and his job is serving the community."

After his police career ended in shame and disgrace, DeAngelo worked at a distribution centre for Save Mart grocery stores for 27 years as a truck mechanic. But by April 2018, that was all in the past.

Now, Joseph James DeAngelo Jr was facing charges of committing a slew of unfathomable, heinous crimes. If convicted, he would surely have a date on California's death row at the infamous San Quentin Prison, joining hundreds of other losers who life had forsaken, or vice versa.

Sitting in a police interrogation room following his arrest, DeAngelo was mumbling to himself and alluding to an imaginary entity called "Jerry". One district attorney later called it "a B.S. act".

DeAngelo mumbled to no one in particular: "I did all that. I didn't have the strength to push him out. He made me. He went with me. It was like in my head, I mean, he's a part of me. I didn't want to do those things. I pushed Jerry out and had a happy life. I did all those things. I destroyed all their lives. So now I've got to pay the price."

Prosecutors would later claim the suspected homicidal maniac was faking a split personality.

"The scope of Joseph DeAngelo's crimes is simply staggering," Sacramento County prosecutor (later the District Attorney) Thien Ho said. "Each time he escaped, slipping away silently into the night."

Playing crazy man was part of the suspect's MO. He tried the same ruse when he was arrested for shoplifting years before. Ho called it "feigned feeble incoherence". While under surveillance, the accused had appeared sharp, Ho noted.

Noted Northeastern University criminologist James Alan Fox said the serial killer as a crazy man is mostly a myth. Most don't struggle with dual personalities, nor are they plagued by inner voices compelling them to kill.

That, Fox said, is the Hollywood template for serial murder, and it is far removed from reality. If DeAngelo truly was criminally insane, he would not have gotten away with his crimes for decades. Most serial killers are organized and cunning, and severe mental illness would render them incapable of escaping detection.

And the murderous alter ego? That's a ruse, too.

"It's self-serving for someone to suggest that they did all of these things because of this voice: 'Don't blame me, blame the voice,'" Fox told ABC News.

Like many post-war American horror stories, the melodrama begins in the east before reaching its violent crescendo west of the Rocky Mountains in the promised land of sunny California.

While the days of terror during the rape and murder epidemic were decades in the past, they were a nightmare without end for the survivors and the people who lived through that frightening era.

"We walked by that house all the time … but we never saw him," Colleen Fernandez told reporters. "I'm just thankful he got caught. It's huge for this community. Even though it was 40 years ago, people still remember."

What Fernandez remembered were nights packed with fear in a very "scary time".

"I was just a young woman. It was frightening. You'd definitely lock your doors and your windows," she said. "You had [a] buddy system. I worked at a restaurant – I made sure somebody walked me to my car."

What detectives and prosecutors faced in the Golden State Killer case was an enigma wrapped in a riddle. A gigantic question mark.

Who was Joseph James DeAngelo Jr? What did his past illustrate about the present? How did this loud, if not innocuous, man become one of the most notorious serial killers in American history? What triggered his bloodlust? And why, in 1986, did he suddenly stop? Or were there more murders that went undetected?

1

Origins of a Killer

What made Joseph DeAngelo a serial killer is a dossier packed with truckloads of speculation, slivers of truth, red herrings and myths.

His birthplace, Bath, New York, in the southern Finger Lakes wine country, is a tiny hamlet of 11,000-odd souls about 100 miles (160 km) southeast of Buffalo, New York. It is the largest community in rural Steuben County.

The population is 96 per cent white and avowedly conservative, its streets lined with tall deciduous trees and stately old homes. There is little noteworthy about the town aside from its annual dairy festival held in June.

It is a Hallmark movie ready. Time moves slowly there. Swap out the modern vehicles and you could easily find yourself back in 1957.

Nearby are the stunning Finger Lakes, a playground for New York City's wealthy for over a century. Corning, where the famed cooling wares originate, is just down the road, as is Watkins Glen, where one of the largest concerts in history was held.

On 28 July 1973, at the Watkins Glen Grand Prix Raceway, more than 600,000 rock fans danced and chilled to the Allman

Brothers Band, the Grateful Dead and The Band. More than 150,000 tickets were sold for the Summer Jam at Watkins Glen, but everyone else entered for free.

And in this corner of New York State, there remain vestiges of the hippy days of yore. Microbreweries, vegan restaurants, and craft and antique stores dot the countryside.

This is where the story of Joseph DeAngelo begins.

Since the first half of the twentieth century, the DeAngelo family has had deep roots in this picturesque corner of the Empire State. The family footprint, however, is light.

The future serial rapist was born in the former Bath Memorial Hospital on 8 November 1945. He is the town's most famous former resident – although there are several notables in the military realm – and only another killer gives him a run for his money in the notoriety department.

Suspected serial killer Richard William Davis was born four years before DeAngelo in Pennsylvania, before his family moved to Bath.

Like his fellow Bath native, Davis, too, flew under the radar for decades until he was posthumously linked via DNA and genetic genealogy to the horrific 7 February 1974 kidnapping and sex slaying of five-year-old Siobhan McGuinness. The little girl had been stabbed to death near Turah, Montana.

Davis had also been linked to an attempted kidnapping of another little girl in Bath in 1973. However, Davis eluded authorities throughout his life and had never been convicted or considered a suspect in any violent crimes while alive.

He died of natural causes at his Arkansas home in 2012, years before investigators would discover his link to any such vile crime.

Homicide detectives have long believed that Davis – who was 70 when he died – was responsible for other violent crimes across the US. He spent much of his life roaming around the country, moving from job to job. In addition to Bath, he lived in Pennsylvania, Alaska, Colorado, Florida, Illinois, Mississippi, Montana, North Dakota, Ohio, Oklahoma, Oregon, Washington and Wyoming.

But by the end of his life, he was a self-proclaimed born-again Christian and a trusted volunteer for the charity group Big Brothers. The organization provides companionship and activities for fatherless boys.

As for Davis, the FBI has said the investigation is continuing into the former Bath resident's murderous trail that spanned decades.

In addition to murder, Davis and DeAngelo had in common that they and their families left few footprints in this veil of tears, particularly in Bath, NY.

His father and namesake, Joseph James DeAngelo Sr, was born in Watkins Glen, NY, on 19 January 1920, the child of Italian immigrants Saverio DeAngelo and Francesca Belvedere. Mother Kathleen DeGroat was born in Elmira, NY, the daughter of Charles and Helen B. DeGroat.

DeAngelo's parents began courting in 1940, although it is unclear how they met. One newspaper article noted that the pair had been involved in a car crash and that Kathleen, then 17, was taken to the hospital with arm, hand and shoulder injuries. Her future husband was driving.

As the storm clouds of war gathered over Europe and Asia and the Nazis steamrolled over the Old World, the young couple married on 20 November 1941 – less than three weeks before the Japanese attack on Pearl Harbor that drew America into the Second World War.

Reverend Joseph D. McDanel of the Elmwood Avenue Baptist Church in Elmira Heights officiated.

But global events ensured the newlyweds' honeymoon would be short-lived. As America entered the deadliest war in human history, Joseph DeAngelo Sr registered for the draft in early 1942. He was inducted into the United States Army Air Force in mid-1942.

Joseph Sr, a top turret gunner on a B-24 Liberator bomber, took part in the famed Operation Tidal Wave against the oil refineries at Ploiești, Romania, on 1 August 1943. The objective was to hammer the Nazis' ability to supply their war machine with oil.

But the attack is regarded by historians as a disaster, with the USAAF losing 53 bombers and more than 500 aircrew who were listed as killed, wounded, captured or missing. Fliers earned five Medals of Honor (the highest US military award for valour) along with countless other medals awarded for courage.

Fliers who took part in the attack were profoundly affected, with many no doubt developing post-traumatic stress disorder (PTSD), which was unheard of at the time. Did those violent hours and losing so many friends affect the way Joseph Sr dealt with his wife and children following the war?

A 1999 report from the US Air War College called it "one of the bloodiest and most heroic missions of all time".

As the war in Europe was winding down, DeAngelo Sr was posted to the Pacific theatre of war.

The Elmira *Star-Gazette* reported that the hometown boy had been wounded in action on 23 February 1944 in air combat over Australia. The *Star-Gazette* noted that Staff Sergeant DeAngelo entered service in April 1942 and was trained at Biloxi Air Base in Mississippi. The paper added that his wife, Kathleen and their 17-month-old baby, Rebecca Louise, resided at 52 East Morris Street in Bath.

Two more children arrived when Joseph Sr returned from the war in early 1945 – his namesake in November of that year, followed by a third child, John Charles, in October 1949.

According to the *Star-Gazette* in a 2019 story, the apartment house where the family lived at 52 East Morris Street was torn down in 2006. In its place now is a parkette.

While Joseph DeAngelo Jr would later make a horrific impression on the world, the killer and his family's tracks are sparse in western New York. It's as if they were never there.

But while some veterans couldn't wait to return to their hometowns following the Second World War, others were ready to leave it all behind and get a fresh start.

Former Bath Fire Chief Joe Washburn told the Elmira *Star-Gazette* in 2019: "No one remembers the guy or the family."

Even Steuben County Historical Society director Kirk House was flummoxed by the mysterious DeAngelo family and its sinister scion. He told the *Star-Gazette* he had spent hours researching the family and their ties to the Finger Lakes area, but traces were scant.

And that means even less information on what trauma or psychosis helped create the Golden State Killer.

"There was a permanent Di- or D'Angelo family in Bath, but we haven't found any connection to that family and the DeAngelos," House said. "People who would have been contemporaneous in school with him have no memory of him."

School yearbooks also provided zeros for the researcher.

And while locals were stunned that one of their own was a serial killer, nothing triggered memories that DeAngelo had ever actually been there.

"I remember reading [about the Bath connection] at the time [he was arrested], and thinking 'I have no idea,'" Bath woman and DeAngelo contemporary Judy Hunter said.

Those missing memories intrigued Steuben County District Attorney Brooks Baker.

"My knowledge comes from the same TV shows that everybody's watching. I was watching that (*Golden State Killer:*

It's Not Over) series on the Discovery Channel when they found the guy," Baker told the Elmira newspaper. "They followed the story back to Bath. [DeAngelo] is about 70, which would put him at the same age as my father and mother, who grew up in the Bath area, and my aunts and uncles and cousins. No one in my family remembers him."

Local reports suggested that records of Joseph DeAngelo Jr's presence in Bath were in lockdown in the Bath Village Clerk's office. And they were not willing to release them.

In his hometown of Bath, NY, after news broke of Joseph DeAngelo's arrest, it raised eyebrows for local law enforcement, along with puzzled expressions.

"He might have done something off-the-wall, or they might have known him as an All-American boy," Brooks Baker said of the young DeAngelo.

Baker said the Steuben County District Attorney's office had not been contacted by California law enforcement officials about DeAngelo, but that there was nothing surprising about that.

"They would reach out to the [New York] State Police or Bath P.D. looking for background information if that was necessary," Baker said. "Based on how we do things here, that would probably be a law enforcement to law enforcement contact. Now, whether there has been some contact from the California Highway Patrol, the FBI and those folks to State Police or Bath P.D., I couldn't tell you."

He added: "People are putting DNA out into the public eye through the internet, and it allows law enforcement to look in a lot more places. It expands our investigations and increases the workload for folks, but it [also] gives us the opportunity to look at a lot more people.

"For them to put together this case across five or six jurisdictions with six or seven law enforcement agencies over a 40-year period, and to come out with a rock-solid suspect and then link it back through DNA is amazing. It's a testament to dogged police work and cooperation. Around here, we're very lucky that our police agencies cooperate within the county, but try to stretch it statewide, and it's amazing that law enforcement is able to do that."

During wartime, many men had become comfortable and acclimatized to being in the military. Many would remain in the service for its stability and steady pay cheque.

At war's end, with his options limited, Joseph DeAngelo Sr would also stay in the service. He appears to have chosen to remain in what would become the United States Air Force, entailing many different postings. One of them was West Germany.

Family lore suggests it was an incident in Cold War Germany that sent Joseph Jr embarking on the dark path his life would take. Several incidents in childhood may have been the impetus for DeAngelo's violent, sadistic streak and ultimately vile contempt toward women.

One family member said it was at an American airbase in the former Fatherland where the trigger was pulled. It was a stomach-churning incident capable of unsettling the strongest person, let alone a small child.

Nephew Jesse Ryland – son of DeAngelo's sister Connie – told *BuzzFeed News* that when the future killer was nine or ten years old, he witnessed his sister being raped by two airmen on the base.

Ryland said that DeAngelo was playing with Connie in an abandoned warehouse on the base when the airmen walked in. Without barely saying a word, they sexually ravaged the tiny girl. All the young Joseph DeAngelo could do was watch in horror as the perverts took turns attacking seven-year-old Connie.

"That's pretty crazy for a kid to see his sister be violated," Ryland said, adding he learned about the incident from his mom just before she died of cancer in 2017. "Maybe that was the start of Joe going wacko."

One expert believes witnessing his sister being raped would be profound for any young boy. It also may have planted the seeds of the depravity that grew like a cancer in DeAngelo.

Ann Wolbert Burgess – a psychiatric nursing professor at Boston College – studied the personalities of 36 convicted serial killers from the late 1970s and early 1980s while working with FBI agents in the Behavioral Science Unit.

Serial criminals, she said, typically develop an obsession with their chosen criminal outlet at an early age. An event like watching your younger sister being raped fits the bill.

"Of course, that would be significant and could have set the nucleus of the fantasy," she said. "What probably happened was that it was something that he kept on his mind."

Ryland added that the DeAngelo children's upbringing was far from the 1950s idyll of white picket fences. For starters, their father was an abusive alcoholic, returning from the battlefield a violent and bitter man.

Besides being abusive to his children, he would frequently batter their mother, Kathleen. She, in turn, physically assaulted her youngest daughter, Connie.

"She would hit my mom all the time," Ryland said, adding that his mother would at times wear two pairs of pants to lessen the blow. "I'm pretty positive they were all abused like that."

Military Police were onto Joseph DeAngelo Sr's domestic terrorism. After yet another beating, he was warned he would be kicked out of the service if he ever touched his wife again.

When the children told their parents that Connie had been raped, both were warned never to discuss it again. The silence was a by-product of the times and Joseph Sr's controlling hand.

No doubt, the incident left both children bewildered.

Burgess believes the incident may have been highly confusing for the future murderer and rapist. The deeply unsettling home life with DeAngelo's parents constantly at loggerheads may have affected his psychological development, she added.

An abusive home life has long been the mark of serial predators. But experts agree: the vast majority of children who grow up in these tragic circumstances don't become killers. Instead, they lead normal lives, find fulfilling work and become loving husbands and parents.

Retired cold case investigator Paul Holes noted that the Golden State Killer would often become infuriated with his victims. He was probably "channelling part of his childhood psychology" into his crimes, Holes believed.

DeAngelo once told his brother-in-law Kenneth Ryland Sr after he got nicked for shoplifting that he stole things simply because he could. "Something like that, and I thought that was really weird," Ryland said. His family noted that something wasn't quite right with "Joe".

Even to those who knew him best, Joseph DeAngelo was a mystery. His nephew said he never saw a violent side, though. Instead, he was nice. A normal guy. What's more, he and Connie were very close.

But when Jesse Ryland heard that his uncle had been arrested and named as the Golden State Killer, things began to make sense, and it raised a slew of troubling questions about the family's dark past.

"Joe was young and saw my mom get raped," he said. "It instantly clicked in my head."

Ryland added that he hadn't seen DeAngelo in more than a decade, even though his mother and his uncle were close.

"I almost wish I could go and see him and ask Joe about it if he remembers," Ryland said, referring to the traumatic childhood incident. "It's probably not a good time for that."

Growing up, DeAngelo and his siblings were service brats moving from post to post in Germany and the US. By the late

1950s, Joseph Sr had been posted to Mather Air Force Base near Sacramento.

Joseph DeAngelo Sr bought one of the prefab homes being built in booming nearby Rancho Cordova, a tiny town of 7,000 souls. In his inimitable style, the patriarch furnished the home with mortgaged furniture, including the children's bunk beds and a radio. The family had arrived in town just in time for Joseph Jr to attend junior high.

But friends never saw Joseph Sr around very much. Eventually, the Air Force posted him to South Korea and then Florida. By that time, the DeAngelos' marriage was disintegrating, and Kathleen and the four children stayed behind in Rancho Cordova.

Bizarrely, Joseph Sr remained in South Korea, remarried and had four more kids – all gifted the same names as his American children.

It remains unclear exactly when the DeAngelos were divorced. Some reports suggest it was 1960, while others are more vague.

Meanwhile, Kathleen had mouths to feed, and she began working as a waitress at Denny's, an American chain of breakfast diners. There, she met a travelling welder from Southern California who was married with children.

Her freewheeling social life did not sit well with her son. Joe Jr's relationship with his mother was filled with screaming matches, mostly over the demands placed on the headstrong young man. With his mother off working or gallivanting with her new boyfriend, DeAngelo was left in charge of taking care of his younger siblings. That included cooking their meals, getting them to school in the morning and washing their clothes.

In 1960, youthful Democrat John F. Kennedy was elected US President over Republican Richard M. Nixon in an electoral squeaker. The new president galvanized young Americans when, on his inauguration day, he implored the nation's youth:

"Ask not what your country can do for you but what you can do for your country."

The call resonated, with many going into the Peace Corps and others entering military service. He was a new president for a new America in a hopeful new era, even though the threat of nuclear annihilation loomed over the planet. In 1962, JFK stared down the Soviet Union over missiles being discovered in Cuba in a diplomatic stand-off that came too close to the edge of Armageddon.

Taking his cue from JFK, after graduation from Folsom High in 1964, DeAngelo followed one of his buddies into the service by enlisting in the US Navy. He had dreamed of flying jets for the naval service, but things didn't turn out that way.

Instead, DeAngelo's dreams of heroism and patriotic glory would be shattered, and the Navy posted him in the galley, preparing food for the ship's crew. Later, he was transferred to a job somewhat less insufferable as a below-deck mechanic, first on the USS *Canberra* and then the USS *Piedmont*.

By 1965, the Vietnam War started to get hot with US President Lyndon B. Johnson finally committing the US Marines for combat in March of that year. That deployment would become a tragically slippery slope. Over the next seven years, hundreds of thousands of soldiers, sailors, airmen and Marines would be sent to the Southeast Asian country, and too many of them were coming home in body bags.

DeAngelo saw none of that action. For the most part, he was stationed on patrol off the coast of North Vietnam in the Gulf of Tonkin. The highlight of his service was when he lost the tip of one of his fingers.

The young sailor would later tell friends and strangers alike that he had lost the tip of his finger while serving on a swift boat on the muddy and extremely dangerous rivers of Vietnam. The truth was he was injured below deck on the ship, safely away from the killing fields of Vietnam.

Instead, DeAngelo would serve two uneventful tours of duty patrolling the waters of the Gulf of Tonkin. He did not sign up for a third hitch and, on 1 June 1967, was honourably discharged with another year to go in the naval reserve.

The young sailor returned to a radically different America than the one he left behind when he sailed from San Diego into the unknown waters of war.

The music was different, the culture was different, men's hair was longer, girls had embraced the pill and free love, and thousands of young people were migrating west to the Promised Land of California, as they had done for decades.

His mother had married her clandestine lover, welder Percy John Bosanko Jr, and they settled in Exeter in farm-filled Tulare County. The tiny town (population: 10,000) sits about halfway between Fresno and Bakersfield in the fertile San Joaquin Valley near the foothills of the Sierra Nevada. After his naval service, DeAngelo returned to live with his mother and her husband in Exeter while he tried to figure out what to do with his life.

One option he had looked at was becoming a cop. The future was a blank page haunted by invisible demons that would soon enough be sprung upon the world.

The distance between Bath, NY, and Citrus Heights, California, is 2,662 miles (4,284 km), 38 hours by car.

But the violent journey travelled by Joseph DeAngelo would feature a dazzling slew of twists and turns over decades. The Golden State is the co-star of his vile horror show.

His California stomping grounds were a fertile field of homicidal possibilities – as it had been for generations.

2

The Golden State

Since gold was struck in 1849, California has been the American promised land, offering a bounty of untold natural riches and possibilities. From the beaches of the Pacific Ocean to the Mediterranean climate of Southern California to the mountains to the stunning redwoods of the north, the state offers stunning geographical features and an agricultural bounty. It has been a magnet for dreamers, chancers, the ambitious, and the bottom dwellers for generations.

Today, it is the largest sub-national economy in the world and the most populous state in the US, with a population of more than 40 million people.

Since that first western migration more than 175 years ago in pursuit of glittery riches, every new generation has believed the streets were paved with gold, literal and figurative, under the hot Pacific sun.

Hollywood and the celebrity culture continue to be emblematic of this. Every day, scores of young men and women get off the bus in downtown Los Angeles or at LAX (Los Angeles International Airport) with stars in their eyes and the certainty that fame and fortune await.

"People come out here to be somebody else," James Ellroy, the crime fiction writer who penned *L.A. Confidential*, told the author in 2006. "When you have that little self-esteem, terrible things are bound to happen."

Many of the rootless migrants who arrived in the state were never able to shake their troubles and familial demons that drove them westward in the first place. These demons have frequently played themselves out in horrifying crimes that have shocked the country and the planet.

In his iconic 1967 book, *Hell's Angels*, author Hunter S. Thompson explains the titular gang's antecedents – and that goes a long way in understanding the violent, sensational nature of California crime.

Thompson described the gang as descendants of bonded servants who drifted west as stragglers of the great western migration. While some migrants settled down into middle-class life after the Second World War, the Hell's Angels were born from those who did not.

Before the war, millions from the Dust Bowl made their way west, as detailed in John Steinbeck's *The Grapes of Wrath*. The old life was left behind in Oklahoma, Arkansas, Kansas and elsewhere. Everything they owned was packed on their backs or in rundown jalopies.

Years of drought ravaged millions of acres of farmland, leaving their past lives untenable. At first, the rumblings of California as the answer to the prayers were a whisper; then they became a roar.

There were jobs picking fruit and other produce in California, which they believed to be a land of milk and honey. Instead, it would be a difficult adjustment in the dire work camps located outside the state's farming communities.

An estimated 400,000 Dust Bowl refugees moved west during the 1930s. Most settled in the Los Angeles area and the San Joaquin Valley.

"Dad bought a truck to bring what we could," former migrant Byrd Monford Morgan said in a 1981 interview. "There were fifteen people to ride out in this truck, in addition to what we could haul."

Another migrant farmer summed it up thus: "1927 made $7,000 in cotton. 1928 broke even. 1929 went in the hole. 1930 went in still deeper. 1931 lost everything. 1932 hit the road."

There was no red carpet for the newcomers, derided as "hillbillies" and "fruit tramps", and no matter where they were from, Californians called them "Okies" (the shorthand term for residents of Oklahoma).

Besides being eyed as a land of hope in the darkness of the Great Depression, young starlets flooded into Hollywood as it entered its golden age of cinema.

With so many rootless people, it was inevitable that violent crime would follow. California crime didn't seem like the kind of homicides cops back east were used to investigating. Murders in the Golden State were more violent, over-the-top and sexualized, whereas in Boston, barflies might squabble over a baseball game, and one ends up dead on the floor with a knife in their chest.

Out west, such a mundane murder might also have a bizarre flourish of some sort or another. And for decades, homicide in California was more violent, more twisted, more evil.

The true story behind the Angelina Jolie blockbuster *Changeling* was a case in point and a chilling harbinger of the nightmare of the serial killer phenomenon to come nearly 50 years in the future.

Gordon Stewart Northcott – born in Saskatchewan, Canada, in 1906 – moved to the Los Angeles area with his parents in 1924. With help from his father, he built a chicken ranch and a house outside Wineville, about an hour east of LA in Riverside County. Also along for the ride was his nephew Sanford Clark, who had recently arrived from Canada.

But besides being a chicken ranch, the property became a house of horrors at the hands of Northcott.

The sex fiend would kidnap boys off the street, take them to the ranch and sexually abuse them. More often than not, Northcott would release the boys near their homes.

At least four of the boys never left the ranch alive, and detectives believed that Northcott had murdered upwards of 20, although they could never muster enough concrete evidence to charge Northcott for all his suspected slayings. He would, however, eventually pay the price.

By the summer of 1928, Northcott knew that the cops were closing in and fled with his mother to their native Canada, where they were arrested by the Royal Canadian Mounted Police on 19 September. Mother and son were returned to Los Angeles at the end of November.

His mother copped to murdering Walter Collins (the subject of *Changeling*), and police didn't pursue Northcott in the matter. But the law wasn't through with Northcott.

Investigators finally did charge Northcott with the sex slayings of underage Mexican national Alvin Gothea, who newspapers of the time called the "Headless Mexican", and brothers Lewis and Nelson Winslow. Lewis was 12, while Nelson was 10 years old. The siblings had vanished from Pomona, California, on 16 May 1928.

In the press, the slayings became known as the Wineville Chicken Coop Murders.

Northcott went on trial in early 1929 in Riverside County. Prosecutors told the jury that the farmer kidnapped, molested and tortured the boys in 1928. He was convicted on 8 February 1929 and sentenced to die five days later. By this time, he had confessed to nine murders.

The serial killer was hanged at the notorious San Quentin Prison on 2 October 1930. In a karmic twist, the rope failed to snap Northcott's neck, and it took him 13 minutes to strangle to death.

Gordon Stewart Northcott would not be California's last serial killer, not by a long shot. There were many bloody decades to come.

Between 1930 and 1940, California's population boomed by 65 per cent, and as it turned out, the timing was perfect. With war clouds hovering over the planet, the Golden State experienced an industrial explosion to support the effort to vanquish Nazi Germany, Imperial Japan and their nefarious allies.

It was fat city for the Okies. Many families who had left the difficult and dirty toil of farming the fields to move to Los Angeles or the San Francisco Bay Area quickly found employment in the booming shipyards and aircraft factories that were gearing up to supply the war effort.

In addition to the job-seeking migrants, the war work available in California triggered another population explosion. And when the bloody conflict finally ended, many migrants who came to work in the factories stayed, drawn by the temperate climate and economic prospects.

Also adding to the state's population explosion were hundreds of thousands of servicemen who looked around and liked what they saw. There was nothing for them back in Allentown, Youngstown, Detroit or Cleveland, so they stayed.

Between 1940 and 1950, the population of California boomed by 53 per cent, making it the fastest-growing area in the United States. The good life was under the golden sun, coupled with stunning vistas. The lure of Hollywood also continued to draw young chancers to the Pacific coast.

But the upheaval of the war years took a toll on the societal fabric. In addition to the factory workers and wannabe movie stars, the era's unrest also brought the troubled, the desperate and the criminally insane to California, particularly Los Angeles.

Under the palm trees and warm sun, murder was in the air. With the influx of people, it stood to reason that among the millions of military personnel and factory workers, some would be homicidal maniacs or people desperate enough to kill.

Los Angeles during the war years and afterwards became a very dangerous place, particularly if you were a woman.

Georgette Bauerdorf was no "fruit tramp" or "Okie" down on her luck. She was a pretty, raven-haired oil heiress born in New York City. But when she was 11 years old, her world was turned upside down by the death of her beloved mother. Her father decided to move the family from New York to Los Angeles for a fresh start.

She attended the posh Westlake School for Girls, where she made many friends. Just after her high school graduation, the US entered the Second World War, and Georgette was a patriotic young woman.

At 20, Georgette lived as many wealthy young women do, but she also volunteered as a junior hostess at the famed Hollywood Canteen. The establishment had been created by movie stars Bette Davis and John Garfield as a spot offering food, dancing and entertainment for enlisted men and women.

It wasn't unusual to see someone like Rita Hayworth dancing with a US Marine sergeant or a sailor from Nebraska. Most of the clientele were en route to the fighting in the Pacific theatre and the very real possibility that they might be coming home in a coffin.

Georgette lived in a luxury two-storey unit at the El Palacio apartments in West Hollywood.

But on the morning of 12 October 1944, the cleaning lady arrived ready to tidy up when she noticed something odd: the front door was open. When she inquired whether there was anyone there, she heard the water running in the second-floor bathroom.

The cleaning woman was greeted with a horrific scene in the bathroom. Lying inside the tub was Georgette, half-submerged in the pinkish water. Initially, cops thought the heiress may have simply tripped and fallen and drowned. However, an eagle-eyed detective noticed the automatic light outside of the unit. Multiple people passed it, but the light didn't click on. Taking a closer look, the cop realized it had been carefully unscrewed several turns to the left, rendering it useless. This pointed to foul play.

The Bauerdorf murder was huge news, so big, in fact, that it pushed the war off page one in newspapers for several days.

Homicide detectives began scouring the dead socialite's private life. That led them to the Hollywood Canteen, where they learned she often gave military personnel the keys to the apartment if they needed a place to crash. They slept on the couch downstairs; she slept in her room.

And she was crazy about men, pals said. Her engagement book was jammed with dinner plans, and when it came to servicemen, she always paid and drove them to restaurants in her sporty Oldsmobile coupé.

Some of her pals thought Georgette was a tad naive, and they warned her to be more cautious about whom she spent time with and the men she let into her apartment. She was indignant: "I think if these boys are willing to fight for us, we ought to do anything we can for them."

On the day before Georgette's body was discovered, she had lunch with her father's secretary and then went shopping. The secretary later told detectives she was excited about a plane ticket she had purchased to see a new soldier boyfriend in El Paso, Texas.

Friend June Ziegler, who saw Georgette at the Canteen, said she appeared happy. Neighbours later said they heard the click-clacking of her luxury high heels. And then, a "crash as if somebody dropped a tray or something". Later – around 2:30 a.m. – another neighbour heard screaming.

"I sat right up in bed and listened," the man told reporters. "It was a feminine voice, screaming, 'Stop, stop, you're killing me.' Then I didn't hear any more, and I decided it was just a family row."

It wasn't. The maid found Georgette naked from the waist down in the tub.

An autopsy revealed that she had fought for her life, suffering abrasions on her hands and face. She had been punched in the head multiple times, with more assaults to her abdomen. Verdict: The heiress died from asphyxiation due to a rag jammed down her throat and had likely been raped.

There was no water in her lungs, meaning the scene was staged to throw detectives off the trail. Her car and $100 were missing, but her expensive jewellery was untouched. The living room floor was littered with cigarette butts. She didn't smoke. Her Oldsmobile was found by police about 12 miles (19 km) away.

The murder victim knew a lot of people, particularly the hundreds of young military personnel who frequented the Hollywood Canteen. The war-bound men were in Los Angeles, and then they were scattered in the wind to the four corners of the earth.

That made for a near-impossible task for homicide detectives.

One bizarre note about the high-profile murder was that the rag found in Georgette's throat was an unusual European-issue medical bandage not used in America for decades. But despite the best efforts of the police, the investigation quickly went cold and remains unsolved.

In a strange twist, one of her acquaintances at the Hollywood Canteen was an attractive young brunette from the Boston area who hoped to be a movie star. Her name was Elizabeth Short.

She is better known in the annals of crime as the Black Dahlia.

A month following the harrowing murder of socialite Georgette Bauerdorf, horror again struck Los Angeles.

On 15 November 1944, the bodies of two mutilated prostitutes were discovered at separate downtown hotels. Victim one was Virgie Lee Griffin, 25, of 1934 West 70th Street. She had been stuffed in a closet in a room at the Barclay Hotel. The tell-tale signs of her cruel fate – a butcher knife and a razor – were nearby. She had been murdered around 8 a.m. and had been slashed and stabbed to death.

Just blocks away, cops were called to another dirtbag hotel around 3:30 p.m. The victim was Lillian Johnson, 38, of 114 West 14th Place. Detectives determined that Griffin and Johnson had been killed by the same fiend. Both had been hacked to pieces, with the injuries inflicted upon Johnson particularly cruel: her breasts and vagina had been dissected.

Patrolman H.E. Donlan scouted the numerous watering holes littering the area.

At a boozer at 326 South Hill Street, just doors away from where Johnson had been slain, the veteran cop noticed that one of the barflies fit the killer's description offered up by hotel staff. In front of him was a glass of wine, next to him was a woman, and he appeared to be moving in for the kill. Perhaps literally.

Donlan noticed the man had in his hand a book of matches from the Barclay Hotel. The copper sidled up to the man and slipped handcuffs around his wrists. The lounge lizard was short-order cook Otto Stephen Wilson, 33, of Nowheresville. He denied any wrongdoing.

But after being interrogated by famed LAPD homicide detective Harry Hansen, Wilson broke under questioning and spilled the beans.

Wilson looked like the film star Robert Taylor. Women liked him, but he didn't particularly like them. His wife had ditched him, with his goodbye kiss being a slash from a razor. He later told detectives he had found the fairer sex too domineering.

Like generations of losers before him, Wilson drifted until he reached the Pacific. There, he got drunk and stayed drunk. He liked being clean-shaven and always carried his straight-blade razor with him. Then he bought a butcher's knife.

Griffin smiled at him in a bar. He smiled back. She told him her husband was away in the service, but she still enjoyed a good time, wink, wink. They decided to hook up and walked across the street to the Barclay.

She told him, "I got my horoscope told. Wednesday is my lucky day."

Inside the room of death, he choked her until she stopped breathing. He had a cigarette and drank a bottle of bourbon and then carved her to pieces. Griffin's body was dismembered beyond recognition.

After the slaying, he walked to the Million Dollar Theater and fittingly watched the Boris Karloff horror film *The Walking Dead*.

Afterwards, he met Lillian Johnson at the Red Front Bar. Same deal, and the pair made their way to the rundown Joyce Hotel, where Johnson met the same fate.

Wilson, in turn, met his end on 9 September 1946 in the gas chamber at San Quentin.

There were other high-profile homicides in California following the bloody autumn of 1944, but none have ever come close to the sheer brutality, mystery and violence of the Black Dahlia murder. It is forever seared into the life of Southern California. A cautionary tale as pertinent today as it was in 1947.

A mother and her child found the 22-year-old's mutilated remains at the corner of 39th and Norton in Los Angeles. It remains America's most notorious unsolved murder.

Elizabeth Short was a wannabe starlet from the Boston suburbs who had drifted west like thousands of other wide-eyed women. She wanted to be a movie star. And she wanted to be loved.

She was a starry-eyed, dark-haired beauty who loved the movies and romance magazines.

On 15 January 1947 – chillier than normal for the Southland – the woman the *Los Angeles Herald-Express* dubbed the Black Dahlia was found cut in two in plain sight.

Her injuries were unspeakably horrific. Short's final hours – cops estimated she was tortured for three days – were filled with pain and terror. The Dahlia had ligature marks on her ankles, wrists and neck. Part of her right breast had been cut off. She had been dissected in half post-mortem and exsanguinated – all the blood had been removed from her body. Her lovely face had been cut into a cruel smile.

The autopsy also noted that Short's anal canal was dilated at 1¾ inches (44.5 cm), meaning she was brutally sodomized. However, there was no presence of sperm.

Generations of LAPD and amateur detectives have tried to unravel the case and expose the monster responsible once and for all. There were hundreds of false confessions cops had to wade through.

And the Black Dahlia herself was a woman of mystery. She was rumoured to be a prostitute or engaged in making pornographic movies, or that she was a lesbian and the killer was a spurned female lover. There is little evidence supporting any of those theories.

The case went cold and haunted LAPD detective Harry Hansen for the rest of his long life.

But because of the horrific and perverse injuries inflicted on Short, detectives always suspected her killer had medical knowledge. In recent years, the spotlight has focused on LA society surgeon George Hodel as the killer.

His son Steve is himself a retired LAPD homicide detective. He thinks his father was the killer.

"The killer had performed a hemicorporectomy on her," Steve Hodel told the *New York Post* in 2019. "It's a unique procedure that was taught at medical school in the 1930s, when he was there, where you cut between the second and third lumbar vertebrae. It's the only way you can divide a body without cutting through bone."

George Hodel was something of an eccentric who was head of the LA County Health Department's hygiene division. His speciality was venereal disease control. Dr Hodel travelled in rarefied Hollywood circles of the time, marrying director John Huston's ex-wife Dorothy, his third go-round at wedded bliss.

Among his close friends was the photographer Man Ray. And he resided in a spacious, somewhat bizarre mansion that was modelled on a Mayan temple.

Steve Hodel says his father knew the Dahlia as a patient and began an affair with her away from his marriage. The former cop remains conflicted about his father.

"I loved my father," he told the New York tabloid. "People say this is a 'Daddy Dearest' thing, but far from it. I was confident I'd be able to show he had nothing to do with these crimes."

Besides the Dahlia, the retired cop believes his father was the maniac behind Chicago's infamous Lipstick Murders. In that horror show, a six-year-old girl was also given a hemicorporectomy.

Wherever George Hodel went, murder seemed to follow. Even his secretary was slain in 1945.

Steve Hodel said he first became convinced of his father's involvement in the heinous crimes when he noticed the handwriting in a letter from the Dahlia killer to the *Los Angeles Examiner*. Detectives always linked George Hodel to the Dahlia murder as well.

In audiotapes from surveillance in the 1950s, the twisted doctor said, "Supposin' I did kill the Black Dahlia. They couldn't prove it now. They can't talk to my secretary anymore because she's dead."

The Black Dahlia case has become the white whale of American homicide investigations and the subject of countless books and movies. The murder has never been solved.

Seventy-eight years after that terrible day in January 1947, there are theories, but still no answers. Yet even with the passage of time, Elizabeth Short remains the quintessential California cautionary tale.

Less than a month after the Black Dahlia snuff, cops had another grisly homicide on their hands that shared many traits with the Short case.

On the morning of 10 February 1947, a bulldozer operator found the naked body of a dark-haired woman lying face up and resting on a red dress and blue coat with fox fur trim. She had had her skull bashed in with a blunt object.

But an autopsy revealed that what caused the victim's departure from this mortal coil was being repeatedly stomped on and beaten by her killer, and that she suffered catastrophic internal bleeding, a broken neck and a punctured heart.

Her twisted killer added a final ghoulish coda to his evil handiwork. Using his victim's bright red lipstick, he scrawled across her torso: "Fuck you P.D." He signed it "Tex". That touch made the murder tabloid ready.

The *Los Angeles Herald-Express* and its successor, the *Herald Examiner*, had mastered the art of naming gruesome homicides with names like the Black Dahlia, the Night Stalker and the Freeway Killer. The maniac who killed 44-year-old Jeanne French would be the "Lipstick Murderer".

Many of the newspapers tried to link French's murder to the film-noir-friendly Black Dahlia slaying. But while the mystery of Elizabeth Short's murder has been eternal, the same can't be said of French's equally squalid demise.

In 1920, she married into Texas oil money but was divorced with a young son four years later. Moving to Los Angeles, she married again before calling it quits after a year. But French was something of an adventuress, learning how to fly and working with a roving band of nurses for an oil company in South America. She married again and then separated five weeks later.

However, for the celebrated "Flying Nurse", by the late 1940s, the world was changing, and she had hit hard times, with the bottle being a frequent companion.

On the night before her lifeless body was discovered, French had dinner and drinks with two strange men at the Plantation Café. One had dark hair and a small moustache, witnesses said.

Staff at the Plantation said by 9:30 p.m., Jeanne was blitzed. She stopped for a coffee at a greasy spoon after leaving the Plantation, before landing at a Venice Boulevard watering hole. French told fellow barflies she was having her abusive factory worker hubby, Frank, committed to an insane asylum.

Around 1:30 a.m., Jeanne sat on a bar stool at the Pan American lounge and guzzled a Seagram's and 7 Up. She asked the piano player to knock out a tune for her.

When the bar closed, she and the "medium-small, dark-complexioned" man were arguing and got into a beat-up sedan. Piano player Sam Young was the last person to see Jeanne French alive.

Cops were hesitant to link the two homicides. They zeroed in on Jeanne's estranged husband, Frank French, who saw heavy fighting as a Marine Corps gunnery sergeant during the Second World War. The pair had a volatile relationship, with violence being the forte of both.

He denied harming his wife and passed a lie-detector test. His landlady confirmed his alibi.

And as in the Elizabeth Short investigation, the Lipstick Murder also went cold. Who was the swarthy mystery man?

"We thought we had this one wrapped up at the start," one homicide detective told the *Herald-Express*. "Now we are just as far from a solution of this one as we are from the 'Black Dahlia."

But some cops believed the same man who murdered Elizabeth Short also killed French. A police document leaked to the *Los Angeles Examiner* named "11 points of Similarity" between the two investigations.

Retired detective Steve Hodel believes his surgeon father not only murdered Elizabeth Short but also Georgette Bauerdorf and Jeanne French. Others are more sceptical.

In the post-war years in California, the economy was booming as servicemen made the difficult transition to civilian life. Things were changing for the Okies as well.

By 1950, only about 25 per cent of the original Dust Bowl migrants were still working the fields. As the former migrants became more prosperous, they blended into the California population and middle-class prosperity.

The Golden State could not have been prepared for the next tidal wave of population and murder.

3

"I Hate You, Bonnie"

When Joseph DeAngelo Jr returned from the Vietnam War on 1 June 1967, the world he had left three years before was rapidly changing. He arrived back in the States just in time for the transcendent "Summer of Love". Change was in the air, on the airwaves, in the movies and the wider culture.

On the day DeAngelo arrived home, the Beatles released their seminal *Sgt. Pepper's Lonely Hearts Club Band* album, which became the soundtrack for the Summer of Love. The album triggered a wave of counterculture copycats and touched on themes like drugs, fashion, mysticism and empowerment. Critics praised the album for marrying pop music and high art.

This was not the soundtrack Joseph DeAngelo had left when he had embarked for Vietnam.

At the movies, the change wasn't quite so seismic. John Wayne and Kirk Douglas starred in *The War Wagon*, a western, and in mid-June, the fifth James Bond blockbuster, *You Only Live Twice*, hit the big screen.

On the little screen, nightly fare would be slow to catch up. Dominating the TV schedules was wholesome fare such as *The Andy Griffith Show*, *The Lucy Show*, dusters *Gunsmoke* and *Bonanza*, *Family Affair*, and ironically, *Gomer Pyle, U.S.M.C.* Of course, the real Gomer Pyle would have been drenched and terrified fighting in the jungles of Southeast Asia.

Belying TV's white-picket-fence worldview of a peaceful happy society, America was at war with itself.

As more American servicemen returned home in body bags or with horrific, life-altering injuries from Vietnam, the country began turning against a war few people understood. Least of all, the young men fighting it or being called to serve.

Protests against the draft were gaining momentum, and it became clear to many working-class and Black Americans that their boys were being called to serve in Vietnam while those of the rich and powerful were not.

If Vietnam was one piece of a fractured puzzle, the civil rights movement was the other. Race riots swept the United States during the so-called "Summer of Love" (1967, when "hippies" in San Francisco demonstrably embraced the ideals of peace, love and freedom). Hardest hit was the home of Motown Records and the US auto industry: Detroit.

The riots kicked off in the early morning hours of Sunday, 23 July 1967. Cops raided an after-hours bar where mostly African Americans were celebrating the safe return of three neighbourhood boys from fighting in Vietnam.

It wasn't the Summer of Love in Motown; it went down as the "long, hot summer of 1967" as tensions between the Black community and the mostly white police force rocketed.

When the five-day riot ended, the National Guard and the US Army's 82nd and 101st Airborne divisions had been dispatched to the riot-wracked city. Forty-three were killed, 1,189 were injured, more than 7,200 arrests were made, and more than 400 buildings were destroyed.

Detroit would never recover. And it wasn't alone.

During the first nine months of 1967, there were more than 150 race riots in America's urban centres. Besides Detroit, rioting hit Newark, New Jersey, where 26 were killed and 700 injured. Milwaukee, Philadelphia, Washington, D.C., New York City and dozens of locales from the Eastern Seaboard to the Pacific coast were hit with unrest.

What this all meant to young veteran Joseph DeAngelo is unclear. But he was a young man seemingly in search of stability. God knows, he didn't find it in his own dysfunctional family.

One childhood friend, who would only be identified as Judy, told the *Los Angeles Times* that the Vietnam vet was yearning for family. He was a friend of her brother's and had followed him into the service. He called the woman's parents "Mom" and "Pop". Judy's family had known DeAngelo since he was a boy, and he was treated like their tenth child.

As kids, DeAngelo and her brother ran wild in tiny Rancho Cordova, where old vineyards and farms were making way for the coming suburban sprawl. They went gigging (spearfishing) for frogs and hunted rabbits with guns. Once, DeAngelo beat up a bully at school.

Her parents went so far as to put his class photo on a mantelpiece alongside pictures of the rest of their big brood. Judy told the *Times* Joe would often nip at a flask of sloe gin and work on cars. He proposed to one of her girlfriends, but she shot him down.

Judy's mom lectured her brother, Joe and other boys about girls and how they should be treated. One thing DeAngelo never, ever discussed was his feelings and his inner emotional life.

It never crossed Judy's mind, living later as a young woman in her parents' Rancho Cordova house during a rash of Peeping Tom activity, that the hooded face she saw at her window one night, paralyzing her with fear, could be DeAngelo. She would later come to suspect that it had been DeAngelo at her window, but she could never be sure.

As the Summer of Love faded into the bitter fall of 1967, rioting continued to roil the home front as an ever-increasing number of young American men came home in body bags.

Nightly news programmes brought the war into the nation's living rooms for the first time, where people could watch American boys being shot to pieces.

It was on the gravel commons at Sierra College in Rocklin, not far from Auburn, where DeAngelo was by this time living with his mother and stepfather, that he first met Bonnie Colwell. She was blonde and pretty but studious and quiet.

A sophomore (second-year high school student), Colwell was just 18 and working as a lab assistant in the school's science department, taking care of rats, snakes, birds and whatever else came through the doors. That fall, she brought a great horned owl and a starling to the commons to practise flying as part of their rehabilitation. The owl grabbed her shoulder while the starling flew out of her hair, then back into it. A stocky young man watched smiling. Bonnie had never seen him before.

He was muscular and walked with energy as he approached the teenager. His name was Joseph DeAngelo, and he was 23 years old and back home in America after two tours of duty in Vietnam. Soon, he was hanging around the science lab and by the end of that first week had asked her out.

There was something different about DeAngelo compared to the boys she knew. He was worldly, confident and had a lot of swagger, she later said.

Friends and family noted that the pair were an odd couple from the very beginning of their courtship. Bonnie liked the soft, artsy sounds of Simon & Garfunkel, while DeAngelo was obsessed with the raunchy, acid-fuelled bombast of the Doors.

But they also noted that DeAngelo was a friendly, considerate, easygoing guy who laughed a lot and welcomed people he'd just met with a big bear hug. In contrast to the hippie vibes permeating college campuses, the former sailor instead harkened to 1950s *Rebel Without a Cause* James Dean-style, favouring jeans, T-shirts and suede ankle boots.

He told his teen girlfriend matter-of-factly that he had lost the tip of his finger to a stray bullet while on patrol with the brown-water navy in the dangerous Mekong Delta of South Vietnam.

School had never been his thing, and Bonnie tutored him, helping DeAngelo get passing grades at Sierra College.

Even though Bonnie's father, Stan Colwell, was a man increasingly at odds with the changing times, he saw Joseph DeAngelo as a throwback to the manly virtues he had grown up with. As a much-decorated Second World War hero who made countless forays behind enemy lines to rescue pilots who had been shot down, he looked favourably on DeAngelo's two tours in Vietnam. He'd been a truant officer before being promoted to principal at a last-chance high school. And while he didn't like the age difference between Joe and Bonnie, he saw the young man's military service as worthy.

Today, Stan Colwell would be called a misogynist. In 1967, he was a man of his times. But the upheaval in society had infected the family home, a farmhouse, with his increasingly outspoken daughter.

Again, it appeared DeAngelo was searching for the family life he had never enjoyed. He became big brother to Bonnie's four younger siblings. He frequently took Bonnie and the kids to the drive-in, packed into his royal blue Road Runner with the ear-shattering engine. Mostly, he hung out with Bonnie and her family, exuding a bittersweet melancholy.

When Bonnie gave him her Del Oro High class ring, he reportedly beamed like a child.

But behind closed doors and away from friends and family, a very different Joseph DeAngelo began slowly emerging. This was the DeAngelo the world would come to know nearly 50 years later. The Doors would go on the record player, and the glint in his eye made it obvious to Bonnie: he wanted sex. She was a virgin, and he seemed utterly "insatiable".

Bonnie later told homicide detectives seeking insight into DeAngelo's mind and crimes that he never forced her into sex. She didn't feel coerced. There were no BDSM activities in the bedroom. No kinky stuff.

However, sexual relations with Joe were exhausting and often painful. And he had the weird quirk of breaking their clinch just as he was climaxing. Minutes later, he would return and continue intercourse, ejaculating again and again. Often he would climax four or five times during a three-hour sex session, she told investigators.

He boasted that he had "trained himself" to control his body. Bonnie's pain, however, didn't appear to move him to slow down in the slightest, she said in 2018.

Once, hot on the heels of a sex encounter, came an engagement ring. There wasn't ever really a formal proposal, Bonnie told the *Los Angeles Times*. No date was set, but there was an engagement notice in the local *Auburn Journal*. It was Joe's firewall against other suitors, particularly the doctors at the clinic where she worked.

For Bonnie, she saw the betrothal was an opportunity to get out from under her father's suffocating influence.

DeAngelo told her he bought the diamond in Vietnam. It was a big half-carat stone way beyond the pay of a sailor or a college student picking up menial jobs as a driver. Her new fiancé told her it had a "perfect" setting, a thin white gold band.

She had big dreams. An honours student, Bonnie hoped that her next stop would be a slot at one of California's prestigious medical schools. However, Stan Colwell wasn't about to sign off on that. Not in 1970. Instead, it was local Sierra College and then a career in nursing.

One of the things that drew Bonnie to DeAngelo was his Vietnam service. Bonnie and her girlfriends often drove to the Alameda Naval Hospital to visit with veterans wounded during their service in Southeast Asia. Joe was part of that, the counter-counterculture.

As for his job prospects, he had his heart set on joining the California Highway Patrol.

But as the engagement went on, Bonnie told the *Times* she was becoming increasingly uneasy about her fiancé. Joe had an arrogant attitude and liked to break the rules and take chances.

DeAngelo was also speeding excessively in his prized Road Runner muscle car and on his Honda motorcycle. He had frightened her half to death on numerous occasions, particularly when they were riding his motorcycle. Her fear seemed to turn him on, and he would frequently push her natural boundaries. Once, a German Shepherd chased them, attacking the bike, but a swift kick from DeAngelo snapped the canine's neck, killing it.

His other passions besides Bonnie and speed were guns, hunting and raising hell. But he also taught her the ins and outs of late-night bullfighting that aired on Spanish TV stations and beamed across the Mexican border.

DeAngelo taught his future bride how to shoot a gun. And she was pretty good at it. On the American River, she blasted a dove out of the sky with a single shot using a Browning rifle Joe had given her. He was delighted. But the blood and guts of hunting were not for Bonnie. Watching the bird die horrified her. Joe pulled out the dove's breast meat and ditched the rest of the carcass.

With Joe, it was a whole new world for the sheltered Bonnie. She became more adventurous, and he encouraged her to scuba dive, although diving into the unknown black wells was not for her.

Like a lot of other things in his life, DeAngelo seemed to revel in breaking the law, which was ironic given his law enforcement aspirations. He frequently trespassed and routinely broke fish and game laws.

One night, the future killer hopped the fence of a missile contractor to poach frogs. He would also illegally spear fish, shoot a vulture for fun and kill deer out of season, dressing the venison in his kitchen. Still, Bonnie stuck with DeAngelo even though she was terrified of being arrested.

"He was the Alpha," she told the *Los Angeles Times*. "He was in charge. It was, I won't say 'My way or the highway,' because there was never the option to choose. I was already committed before there was an option to choose.

"I just sort of had to throw my trust with him in many situations where I was initially uncomfortable with the choices he made."

But it wasn't the relentless sex drive, the dangerous antics or the lawbreaking that torpedoed the couple's relationship. In many ways, it was the proverbial straw that broke the camel's back.

Never a strong student and often in need of Bonnie's tutoring, DeAngelo was academically struggling in the spring 1971 semester. Both were juniors at Cal State Sacramento, and he was flunking Abnormal Psychology, a mandatory credit if he wanted to graduate from the criminal justice programme.

DeAngelo asked Bonnie to help him cheat. She said no. Her parents were teachers after all. She considered the request disgraceful.

Bonnie knew her boyfriend of three years well enough to know he would still try and cheat by cribbing answers from her test because they were in the same class. She moved her desk away from him.

Joseph DeAngelo would not let the matter rest, nor did he respect – or understand – Bonnie's reasoning. After all, he believed, she was his future wife; it was her obligation to help him cheat. After her refusal, he would bring the subject up nonstop, "pressing harder and harder". And as he intoned that

Bonnie was to fall into line, his voice would become lower and more menacing.

Finally, she decided she had had enough. A meeting was called, and he was asked to meet Bonnie at her father's house. Bonnie told DeAngelo that it was over. They were Quitsville.

"But I love you. We're meant to be together," she recalled him protesting. "We're perfect together."

"We're not a good fit," she said. "I've already decided."

And with that, she gave him back the spectacular white gold ring with the big diamond.

There was no hiding the hurt and disappointment on the face of Joseph DeAngelo. On his way out the door, the devastated young man tossed the diamond into the grass behind the Colwell home. After he drove away, Bonnie and her siblings desperately searched for the ring, but it could not be found.

Later, they concluded that DeAngelo had dramatically staged tossing the bauble.

Just days later, Bonnie saw her ex-fiancé in psych class. He was holding hands with another girl, but if she thought that DeAngelo had thrown in the towel on the relationship, she had another thing coming.

Several nights later, she was startled by a tapping on her window. It was DeAngelo – and he was pointing a gun at her face.

"Get dressed," he ordered. "We're going to Reno."

Something deep in Bonnie told her she was in grave danger, and she sprang from her bed, sprinting down the hall to her parents' room. She awoke her war-hero father.

Bonnie told her dad: "Joe is outside and he has a gun and he wants me to go to Reno with him and marry him right now!"

Stan Colwell had faced the Nazis. He was not afraid of Joseph DeAngelo or much else. He instructed his daughter to lock herself in the bathroom and to wait until he told her the coast was clear. For two hours, Bonnie waited sobbing in the bathroom, pumped with adrenaline and terror. And then Stan Colwell returned.

He told his daughter, "You can go back to bed. Joe's left."

For the Colwell family, the events of that evening in the spring of 1971 became the stuff of legend – and mystery. What did Stan Colwell say to DeAngelo?

For one thing, he didn't call the cops. He never said why he chose not to.

The family believes such a call would have landed DeAngelo in handcuffs, shattering his dream of becoming a cop. Bonnie said she and her father never spoke about the incident again. None of the other five people in the house were aware of the frightening drama.

But the incident left deep scars on Bonnie, and she dropped out of school for a semester. She was terrified of Joe and what he might do. She also switched her major to laboratory sciences.

Several years later, DeAngelo would buy a house less than two miles (3 km) away from the house where Bonnie and her new husband lived. She had married an accountant in 1972. The couple would later divorce.

In 1973, DeAngelo graduated with a degree in criminal justice and was hired as a probationary police officer in the Sacramento suburb of Roseville, where he had spent most of his childhood.

Bonnie would only see Joseph DeAngelo Jr once more before his name exploded over the front pages and airwaves of California and the nation decades later. At a local mall, Bonnie, by now nine months pregnant, could identify the gait from a mile away. It was Joe DeAngelo. She was shopping with her new husband and later said she pulled her husband into a store to hide.

It wasn't until DeAngelo was arrested on 24 April 2018 that his name re-entered Bonnie's well-ordered world.

She was at her home in Italy, helping two American friends navigate the country's train system, when the blast from the past arrived with the emotional weight of an atomic bomb. The phone rang. It was Bonnie's ex-husband.

He asked, "What was the name of the guy you dated before me?"

"Do you mean Joe DeAngelo?" Bonnie replied.

"Yeah, that's the one," her ex-husband said, adding that the county prosecutor had contacted him. "I need to let you know they are arresting him as the East Area Rapist."

A little less than a year after Bonnie and DeAngelo parted ways, there had been reports in the police blotter section of the local newspaper. Cops in Rancho Cordova were receiving reports of what appeared to be a cat burglar or prowler.

Sometimes the suspect at the windows of homes wore no pants. The mystery man also began slipping into bedrooms and touching the women sleeping in their beds. If they woke up, he ran. These nocturnal excursions offered little loot: coins, rings, keepsakes. The incidents seemed to come in waves, sometimes two or three events a night.

But the suspect was also killing family dogs in the area.

Joseph DeAngelo was just getting started. By the end of his reign of terror, he would be in the pantheon of American serial killers. And he would have eluded cops for more than four decades.

In Sacramento and the Bay Area he was called the Cordova Cat Burglar, the Visalia Ransacker, the East Area Rapist, the Creek Bed Killer, the Diamond Knot Killer, the Night Stalker.

He murdered women and he murdered men. Dogs were fair game, too.

His attacks became horror movies unto themselves, frequently lasting hours. An insatiable sexual monster who repeatedly raped and sodomized his victims. The men would be tortured.

This animal's cruelty knew no bounds.

Children would be locked in their bedrooms while the phantom raped their mothers again and again. He bound the men and placed them face down on the floor with a teacup and saucer on their backs and a sick promise. If the cup fell off their backs, the attacker would slice off the ears of their wives or girlfriends.

During the suspect's 37th home invasion, on 6 July 1978, in Davis, California, something odd would unfold that left investigators scratching their heads for meaning.

After repeatedly raping and sodomizing his female victim, the suspect suddenly, inexplicably broke down and began sobbing into the pillow on the woman's bed. He had already threatened to murder her children.

She told cops the man then began uttering something bizarre.

"I hate you, Bonnie," the woman told detectives. "I hate you, I hate you, I hate you."

4

The Golden Age of Serial Killers

California has, for decades, had the reputation of being a "good" place. And it has proven to be a "good" place for serial murderers – a New Jerusalem, a Nirvana, a Valhalla, an Elysian Fields for the vile and demented.

Killers in the Golden State get the headlines in part because of the entertainment-industrial complex. Think O.J. Simpson and other ready-made sensational atrocities, from sex cults to Scientologists to pure homicidal violence.

The West Coast is also a target-rich environment with armies of immigrants toiling in the fields of the San Joaquin Valley while others attempt to become Tinseltown princes or princesses. Chancers whose luck has run out in a thousand other low-rent towns come by in their thousands to roll the dice in California. Effectively, America's last-chance saloon.

Rootless dreamers whose disappearances may not even be noted. John and Jane Does, nameless and unloved, lying in the county morgue.

"There's a socioeconomic pattern to the distribution of serial murder," David Wilson, a professor emeritus of criminology at Birmingham City University in the UK, told *Newsweek*. "If I think about the states which have high concentrations of serial murder victims, they would be places like California, Texas.

"Those states have historically had patterns of indigent workers, immigrant workers coming into the state and not really having roots in the state and therefore if they are murdered, if they disappear, it is often the case that they won't be reported, their disappearance won't be reported to the police."

He added, "Often serial murderers will prey on those people who are somehow for whatever reason seen as living outside of the norms, the moral norms of mainstream culture. So for example there are high percentages of sex workers who are predated by serial killers, high numbers of gay men.

"Again, these are cultural phenomena rather than anything to do with, you know, serial killers. What serial killers do is expose vulnerabilities in our culture because it's those people who are vulnerable to attack by serial killers that tell us about our social organization."

Studies say the golden age of the serial killer was between 1950 and 2000. The first prominent monster to emerge in the 1950s was timid and ineffectual Harvey Glatman. Part pervert, part conman, Glatman was the creep from central casting.

Today, we would peg Glatman as the kind of nerd who spends his days and nights in his mother's basement. Women? Out of the question.

The Glatman grift of perversion was a simple one that played on the hope and desperation of Southern California. Los Angeles has always been full of desperate women who soon discover that their names will not be on the marquee alongside the handsome leading man of the moment, be it Brad Pitt or Cary Grant. Many drift into prostitution and pornography, desperate to comb together a few bucks.

Enter Glatman. Placing notices in the want ads, he sold aspiring models on the premise he'd get their photos placed in the bondage-heavy popular true crime magazines of the era. And, in Los Angeles, there was no shortage of pretty girls waiting to be "discovered".

During the photo shoots, he'd tie them up, gag them and then murder them.

Glatman was born in the Bronx in 1927 and moved to Denver as a kid. An IQ test revealed the young, bespectacled man was very bright, but there were troubling aspects to his personality. From the time he was 12, Glatman showed signs of antisocial and sadomasochistic tendencies. Once, he tied a string around his penis and pulled it to get a sexual thrill. The family doctor claimed he'd "grow out of it".

By the time he was a teen, the budding predator was breaking into women's apartments and stealing lingerie. Naturally, this escalated to rape, and in August 1945, he was busted and sentenced to five to ten years in the reformatory.

When he was transferred to the Big House – Sing Sing, up the Hudson River from New York City – the prison headshrinker described him as a "psychopathic personality – schizophrenic type having sexually perverted impulses as the basis of his criminality".

Sprung in 1948, cops now believe Glatman ramped up his twisted fantasies in 1954. Kids found a woman's body, stripped of clothes and jewellery and dumped in Colorado's Boulder Canyon. For decades, the luckless victim was known only as "Jane Doe 1954".

Fifty-four years later, she was identified as an 18-year-old woman from Phoenix named Dorothy Gay Howard. She lived blocks away from Glatman's childhood home. At the time, he was working as a TV repairman, a convenient ruse for a rapist or killer.

Like many other Americans, Glatman saw California as the golden land of opportunity in the post-war years, a target-rich environment for his sickening schemes.

He quickly set about his vile calling. Using newspaper lonely hearts columns and ads looking for models, this was the conduit to how he satisfied his sick desires. The bodies would be dumped in the nearby desert. On 2 August 1957, he kidnapped and murdered Judy Dull. Shirley Bridgeford was reported missing on 3 March 1958. Ruth Mercado, AKA Angela Rojas, was reported missing on 29 July 1958.

Next on Glatman's death list was a young model named Lorraine Vigil. On 27 October 1958, Glatman attacked Vigil in his car, but she wasn't going to go down without a fight. The gangly Glatman struggled to subdue Vigil, and she managed to get his gun and hold him at gunpoint until a member of the California State Patrol arrived.

After cops busted Glatman for the trio of Southern California murders, they discovered a toolbox in his apartment. It was filled with detective magazines and his horrifying collection of trophy photos. His three LA victims were identified; others were not.

On 18 September 1959, Glatman went into the green-walled gas chamber at San Quentin and never came out. And that was that.

"Harvey Glatman was a pioneer of sorts," author Michael Newton wrote. "Nine years before author John Brophy coined the term 'serial murder', nearly two decades before FBI agent Robert Ressler dusted it off and made the tag a global household word, Glatman was already plying his trade … Glatman never had a catchy nickname [but would] become the stuff of urban myth, a quintessential bogeyman."

While Glatman may have been a "pioneer" in serial murder, as Newton writes, he also paved the way for generations of other killers afflicted with bloodlust.

Following in the pop bottle glasses-wearing Glatman's path would be luminaries like the Zodiac Killer, hippie cult kingpin

Charles Manson, Richard Ramirez (AKA the Night Stalker), the Hillside Strangler, a multitude of "Freeway Killers", the Skid Row Slasher – and Joseph James DeAngelo Jr, the Golden State Killer.

The exact number of serial killers who have operated in California remains a mystery, in part because some killers have never been caught, and the opinions about who fits the definition of a "serial killer" versus a "spree killer" label often vary. Yet, there's still a long list of cold-blooded killers who have been identified over the years and are linked to some of the state's most disturbing murders.

In his seminal book *American Serial Killers: The Epidemic Years 1950-2000*, author Peter Vronsky described a perfect storm of factors that creates a homicidal maniac. Above all, this compulsion needs a sexual fantasy incubator.

One aspect was a violent family heritage inherited by one generation after another, "each crippling its young, leaving behind, at best, a crop of abused and maladjusted individuals, or at worst, a series of raped and dead murder victims".

Vronsky cites society-wide traumas such as the Great Depression, World War Two, and the proliferation of true detective magazines whose lurid covers frequently featured women in bondage. Vronsky called it "transgressive scripting" for domination fantasies. These "indulgences" would twist a generation of boys with the "repressively sick celebration of women's abduction, rape, mutilation and murder".

The Bay Area got a taste of what was to come in the late 1960s when the infamous Zodiac Killer began terrorizing Northern California. Nearly 60 years after the murders, his identity is a mystery but still the subject of widespread speculation and theories.

Zodiac wasn't a sex killer, and whatever dark demons drove him to murder are vague at best. His victims were often young couples whom he gunned down or stabbed to death in the area's lovers' lanes. The bizarre description of the murderer captured the public's imagination – and fears. He taunted cops and the public with missives to the local newspapers featuring complex ciphers.

Cecilia Shepard, who later died of her injuries, provided the description. Her boyfriend, Bryan Hartnell, was killed during a picnic in 1969. She told detectives the mysterious killer was wearing a medieval-style executioner's hood.

Cops would eventually pin five murders on the Zodiac, committed between December 1968 and October 1969. The attacks occurred in Benicia, Vallejo, unincorporated Napa County, and San Francisco proper. He attacked three young couples and a lone male cab driver. Just two would survive.

In his missives, Zodiac claimed he was collecting slaves for the afterlife and vowed bloody vengeance if the papers didn't print them. And then the murders stopped.

His final letter in 1974 claimed his death tally was at 37. Zodiac also boasted that he murdered Cheri Jo Bates in Riverside in 1966. Former elementary teacher and convicted sex offender Arthur Leigh Allen was the only suspect ever named by investigators, but he's not talking – he died in 1992.

Like the Zodiac, Juan Corona's murder rampage was not driven by sexual fantasies. In 1971, the authorities discovered the bodies of 25 migrant farm workers buried in the peach orchards along the Feather River in Sutter County, California. For a brief two-year stretch, he was the deadliest American serial killer. Only Dean "The Candyman" Corll's homicidal rampage in Houston that left nearly 30 young boys dead carried more casualties.

Corona slipped into the US from Mexico in 1950 when he was 16. By 1956, he had been committed to the DeWitt State Hospital in Auburn, California, where he was diagnosed with "schizophrenic reaction, paranoid type". Three months later, he was declared cured and deported to Mexico.

Somehow, the monster in the making got a green card in 1962 and legally entered the US. He was known on the farms where he toiled as a hard worker, but he wasn't without issues. There were periodic schizophrenic episodes and volcanic explosions of temper.

In 1971, he snapped and began his murderous spree, hacking his victims to death with a machete and then dumping their bodies. He was locked away in prison until his death behind bars in 2019.

While Corona's and the Zodiac's murderous impulses weren't triggered by sexual compulsion, the large majority of California serial killers' bloodlust was driven by a cocktail of sex and hatred.

As the "Me Decade" wore on, a small army seemingly from the depths of hell began hunting across the state, killing the feel-good California vibe forever. No one was more aware of the carnage unfolding than the cops.

A daily roster of dead bodies littered the highways, byways, and back alleys of California. Not just one Charles Manson, but many. Each one seemingly more maniacal than the last.

In the 1970s, Los Angeles became the serial killer capital of the world. At least 20 homicidal maniacs – including five at one time – turned LA into a palm tree-filled killing field.

"There is no question Southern California was in a state of panic. We would always say, 'please God, not another one.' Forty-four years later, I still have dreams about the victims and I still want to say, 'don't open that door,'" retired LAPD homicide detective Bob Grogan told the *Toronto Sun* in 2021.

During this dark era, the LAPD investigated more than 100 prostitute murders in ten years.

At the time, in the 1970s and 1980s, there was no DNA testing. No cellphones. Few computers that could do anyone any good. And week by week, in the California dreamscape, the terror spread.

"It finally all came to a head with the Night Stalker," retired detective Bob Souza said of Satanic killer Richard Ramirez's 31 August 1985 capture. "It was a turning point, it all kind of stopped."

The Night Stalker handle was pegged to Ramirez by the now-defunct *Los Angeles Herald Examiner*, a newspaper that specialized in giving Southern California's killers lurid monikers.

As with the Golden State Killer, myriad jurisdictions across California made police coordination difficult. In Los Angeles, there was not just the LAPD but also the LA County Sheriff's Department and numerous smaller police departments in the Southland.

"The problem was communication, and that's something I worry about today. In the old days, we would meet our colleagues in other departments for a coffee in the morning or a beer in the evening," retired detective Tom Lange said.

"You had a better read what was going on when you met face-to-face rather than a stranger sending an email. Today, they're well-intentioned but a different breed. We'd have to keep a roll of quarters and keep our eyes peeled for a phone booth."

But miraculously, through round-the-clock work, teamwork and old-fashioned gut instincts, the detectives got the job done. It wasn't easy.

Kenneth Bianchi and Angelo Buono collectively became the Hillside Strangler. The tag team terrorized Los Angeles between October 1977 and February 1978. The cousins from Rochester, NY, posed as cops and would lure teen girls and young women to their deaths, but not before a cornucopia of sickening depravity was inflicted upon them.

The corpses were dumped along the numerous hillsides dotting Los Angeles. At that time, cops in Southern California were dealing with multiple serial killers with multiple modi operandi. The Hillside Strangler victims were, of course, strangled to death.

A psychic from Berlin offered his help, suggesting that detectives should be hunting two Italians, maybe brothers or cousins, in their mid-thirties. Famed LAPD detective Bob Grogan didn't buy it. But the oracle wasn't far off, and investigators soon believed the Strangler was, in fact, two people.

The first two victims, two prostitutes, were discovered naked on the hills northeast of LA, and both had been strangled to death. But the killers' next five victims were not sex workers but from middle-class neighbourhoods, which sparked major media attention, particularly with the *Herald Examiner* dubbing the maniac the "Hillside Strangler".

Two more homicides followed in December and January. Then, just as quickly as the killings began, they stopped. The murders were headed for the icebox via the cold case warehouse.

But Bianchi got himself pinched in January 1979 for the murders of two young women in Washington state. He was then linked to the Strangler probe. It later emerged that he was a cop wannabe who attended police gatherings where he would ask about the Strangler investigation.

After he was arrested, Bianchi pointed the finger at his cousin, Angelo Buono. The pair were convicted in tandem of the kidnapping, rape, torture and murder of ten women, ranging in age from 12 to 28. Bianchi notched two more kills solo. The killer cousins were convicted and sentenced to life in prison.

Understanding serial killers remains a wander through a particularly puzzling maze. Peter Vronsky in his tome believes wounded fathers resulted in wounded boys who became twisted by true detective magazines that were a "repressively sick celebration of women's abduction, rape, mutilation and murder".

Before Ted Bundy went to the electric chair, he claimed porn had profoundly affected him and driven him to kill. Other serial killers confessed that the effect of seeing barely clad, terrified damsels in bondage affected them and created dark obsessions that would morph into murder.

But not every man who looks at a skin magazine or watches porn becomes a serial killer. Very few do. Vronsky said the lurid crime magazines offered "some kind of powerful primordial male reptilian euphoria" culminating in an unquenchable desire to dominate women by any means necessary.

During the first four decades of the last century, around 200 serial killers were documented. They just weren't called that.

Vronsky described the stereotype for this breed of monster as "often odd or twitchy, Scripture-quoting, rootless, migratory, shabby outsiders; sick refugee flagellant drifters with indiscernible specks of dried blood on the cuffs of their soiled shabby pants".

Men like Harvey Glatman or the fictional child killer Hans Beckert, played by Peter Lorre, in Fritz Lang's classic 1931 serial killer movie, *M*.

But by the late 1970s, the serial killer was ubiquitous in both popular culture and stark reality. As a result, the Federal Bureau of Investigation established its Behavioral Science Unit. Even as understanding of these killers broadened, the slaughter continued.

There were the Toolbox Killers, Lawrence Sigmond Bittaker and Roy Lewis Norris, known for raping young women and then torturing them using a variety of horrendous implements.

Freeway Killer William Bonin traipsed around the highways of Southern California, trolling for boys in his rundown van. Sometimes Bonin killed alone. Other times, he had an accomplice. Between 1979 and 1980, Bonin sexually assaulted, tortured and then killed his victims before dumping their bodies along the freeway.

Bonin was convicted of murdering 14 young men and boys, but investigators believe his true tally includes 15 more victims. Bonin was executed by lethal injection in the green room at San Quentin in 1996.

The Doodler – who remains unidentified – targeted gay men in San Francisco. He got that handle because one of the survivors told detectives he was drawing on a napkin when they met, adding he was a student at a Frisco art school. The killer has been linked to at least five homicides.

And California has had twice as many serial killers as its nearest rival, Texas. Many veterans of the Second World War settled in its sunny climes, which may be the genesis of the slaughter.

Vronsky said he believes the rise of the North American serial killer in the late twentieth century can be traced to the greatest conflict in human history, which lasted six long years, from 1939 to 1945. The future serial killers were the children of men who had witnessed unspeakable horrors in the Pacific and European theatres of war.

"Serial killers come from among us – they come out of our society," Vronsky wrote. "These are not aliens that arrive from another planet. They're children who grow up to become these serial offenders."

But when the soldiers, sailors, airmen and marines returned home, few spoke of what they had witnessed. Instead, they turned inward or to the bottle. This was before PTSD was recognized, and returning veterans were expected to suck it all up, become the man in the grey flannel suit and settle in behind a white picket fence.

"[The war] was far more vicious and primitive than we have been able to acknowledge," Vronsky said, adding that many serial killers have said their fathers returned from combat traumatized.

There was also an uptick of serial murder following the First World War between the years 1935 and 1950, but nothing like what emerged in the 1970s.

Still, the vast majority of veterans returning from war became good husbands and fathers, and even the children of men traumatized from combat grew into emotionally healthy adults, as do most children from broken or impoverished homes.

Researchers noted that serial killing began rising in the late 1960s before hitting its peak in the 1980s, when there were an estimated 200 of these maniacs on the loose in the US.

James Alan Fox, a criminology professor from Northeastern University in Boston, said serial murder climbed at the same time as a general increase in violent crime in the US and Canada. Societal upheaval and widespread hitchhiking offered would-be killers a welcoming environment ripe for murder.

"It just created an environment which was ideal for certain killers to prey on victims," Fox said.

In addition to the Hillside Strangler, other murderers found the Golden State's extensive highway system and the thousands of young hitchhikers an overwhelming temptation.

Trash Bag Killer Patrick Kearney stalked the roadways and gay bars, looking for young men. After the pickup, he tortured his victims and mutilated their bodies before stashing their remains in trash bags. The tragic dead would then be dumped alongside the freeways, landfills and deserts that dot the landscape. Kearney copped to murdering 35 people but only pleaded guilty to 21 slayings.

Like Kearney, Randy Kraft – AKA the Scorecard Killer – targeted young men. He got that grim moniker after he was pulled over by a California Highway Patrol officer in 1983. In the passenger seat was a dead male. In addition, detectives found what they called a "coded list" with the details of 67 victims. Kraft was convicted of 16 murders – young males in Southern California and Orange County – and sentenced to death. He had lured victims into his car with offers of booze and drugs.

Kraft, now 80, remains on death row.

During those dark years from 1950 to 2000, there was a plethora of serial monsters using California as their playground of death. And cops were up against the wall.

Homicide detectives lacked databases that would help connect the dots. DNA testing was years away, and in law enforcement circles, too often, the left hand didn't know what the right hand was doing. Research into these calculating killers was also lacking.

How far behind was law enforcement? The term "serial killer" didn't emerge until the early 1980s.

"The offenders certainly had a head start," criminologist Michael Arntfield said, adding the post-war years triggered a "major upheaval … in society".

"The surge in suburbs and the complete makeover of the demography of the country lead to a lot of transience, a lot of mobility, a lot of broken families, which is where many of these people came from," he said.

The growing Interstate Highway System and myriad freeways linking towns across California gave people greater freedom of movement and allowed murderers to slip away into the night, unseen.

Some experts believe media attention helped fuel many of the killers' bloodlust. But for every monster who leads the nightly news, there are scores of others who are quickly forgotten. Their methods and motivation deviate from the template.

Old Dorothea Puente is a case in point. Puente operated a Sacramento boarding house in the 1980s and 1990s. Her false front was one of compassion and caring. Puente would extend a warm hand to alcoholics and the homeless who lived in her neighbourhood. Once the victims were under her control, Puente gained access to their Social Security benefits.

When they had outlived their usefulness, she would kill them and cash in their benefits. Puente would then bury the victims in the backyard of her Victorian home. She was charged with nine murders and convicted of three. Puente died in prison in 2011.

Chester Dewayne Turner preyed upon sex workers, the homeless, drunkards and drug addicts in the decrepit downtown Los Angeles neighbourhood of Skid Row in the 1980s and 1990s. By the conclusion of his rampage, 14 women were dead. They had been raped and then strangled to death. Cops found one of the bodies just 50 feet from Turner's doorstep.

Turner went down in 2007 for the murders of ten women and was sentenced to death. Seven years later, he was convicted of four additional murders. And in 2024, law enforcement in Utah linked him to the violent cold case murder of Itisha Camp, who was found strangled to death with a scarf in 1998.

Survivalists Leonard Lake and Charles Ng acted as a tag team of terror. Lake was a troubled Vietnam War vet, while Ng had been booted out of the US Marines, and somehow they found each other. At Lake's cabin in rural California, the pair fulfilled their violent rape-and-torture-fuelled fantasies. At least 11 victims were subjected to their heinous paraphilias.

Before death, the victims were kept as sex slaves in the pair's hidden bunker. Lake and Ng recorded their vile acts on video.

Lake was nabbed in 1985 and killed himself in jail with a hidden cyanide capsule. His younger companion went on the run and was later arrested in Canada and then extradited to the

United States. Ng was convicted and sentenced to death. He remains on death row.

Serial killing in California reached its nadir in 1984 and 1985 in the person of a Satan-worshipping lunatic from El Paso, Texas, named Richard Ramirez. Again, the *Los Angeles Herald Examiner* stepped up to the plate to sear Ramirez's vile crimes into our collective consciousness forever.

He was initially called the Walk-In Killer. But during a boozy, informal editorial session at a watering hole near the newspaper's headquarters, the *Herald* editors came up with a better tag.

They called him the Night Stalker.

Ramirez terrorized Southern California and San Francisco for more than a year. His calling card was Satanic symbols left at murder scenes alongside the mutilated bodies. One of his victims' eyes was gouged out, and another was nearly decapitated.

They were men, women, old, young, white and non-white. Some were sexually assaulted, others were not.

What the Night Stalker lived for was seeing the terror in his victims' eyes as he was about to end their lives.

Ramirez's homicidal rampage reached its peak in the broiling summer of 1985. Slipping into homes via unlocked windows and doors, the Night Stalker killed with shotgun blasts to the head and knives to the throat. When his grisly work was concluded, he frequently fixed himself a snack from the victim's larder and stole whatever he could find.

A sense of panic reverberated throughout Southern California. Guns, attack dogs and security systems became de rigueur. And still the murders continued.

Sometimes he would snatch children from their beds, whisk them away to his dingy lair and sexually assault them. Then, bizarrely, he would drop them off near their homes at gas stations and tell them to call their parents. He sometimes ordered victims to "swear to Satan" and painted pentagrams on the walls of the death houses.

One man was murdered in his bed and Ramirez raped his wife beside her husband's lifeless body.

The killer was finally nabbed when police released his photo and name. That chilling photo was on the front page of every newspaper and the lead story on the numerous newscasts in LA.

Ramirez was cornered in a blue-collar neighbourhood in East Los Angeles by gutsy residents who would have torn him limb from limb if police had arrived any later. The Night Stalker was foiled in a botched carjacking and was badly beaten for his troubles.

Even for Los Angeles and California, Ramirez's trial was a circus. Dressed in black, he walked into the courtroom in his first appearance and raised his hand with a pentagram drawn on it and yelled, "Hail, Satan!"

In the lead-up to and during his year-long trial, Ramirez bizarrely became a weird object of desire for not-quite-right girls and women everywhere. They sent him nude photos and love letters, and many showed up daily in Los Angeles Superior Court for a glimpse of the homicidal heartthrob. Ramirez would smile and flash a gesture to his groupies.

But that didn't save him. He was convicted of 13 murders and sentenced to death. Cops have always believed there were many more victims.

In a demonic twist, the trial was nearly aborted towards the end when one of the jurors was murdered during deliberations. She was found beaten and shot to death at the home she shared with her boyfriend. The man committed suicide the next day and left a note saying he had killed her in an argument. The murder had eerie similarities to the Night Stalker killings.

After the conviction, Ramirez flashed a two-fingered "devil sign" to photographers and muttered a single word: "Evil."

In 1987, the Night Stalker's DNA linked him to the horrific murder of nine-year-old Mei Leung on 10 April 1984. She was killed in the basement of a residential hotel in San Francisco's Tenderloin neighbourhood, where she lived with her family not far from the dives where Ramirez lived.

"The Richard Ramirez case was the most difficult trial I ever handled. It was an experience I will never forget, and I'm glad the ordeal is over," Judge Michael Tynan said in 2013 following the Night Stalker's death from liver failure.

Others would follow Ramirez into the Golden State Serial Killer Hall of Fame.

Men like Lonnie David Franklin Jr – AKA the Grim Sleeper – and Samuel Little.

Franklin got the tag Grim Sleeper for the long lag time between his horrific killing sprees. The murders started in the 1980s when multiple women were shot to death with a .25-calibre handgun. Their bodies were then dumped in greasy Los Angeles alleyways and dumpsters.

One victim survived and gave cops a description of her wannabe killer. And then for the next two decades, the killer lay dormant until another woman was discovered in a dumpster in 2007. That discovery linked the Sleeper to a slew of other slayings in the early 2000s. Franklin was arrested in 2010, convicted of murdering nine women and sentenced to death. The Sleeper pegged out in 2020 while still caged on death row.

Samuel Little is an altogether different matter. In some ways, the Cleveland native fits the public's template of how a serial killer operates: The itinerant monster crisscrossed America murdering sex workers, homeless women, alcoholics and junkies.

Dubbed by the FBI as "the most prolific serial killer in US history", Little's killing fields spanned from California to Florida.

He ultimately confessed to killing 93 people. According to the FBI, 50 of those murders have been verified, but investigators have reason to believe that all the confessions were credible.

Although he spent time behind bars for other crimes, he was not linked to any murders until 2012, when his DNA was matched to the 1989 murders of Audrey Nelson and Guadalupe Apodaca in Los Angeles.

It would take until 2018 for Joseph James DeAngelo Jr to join the marquee of madness, but join it he would.

The ultimate question remains: Where do serial killers come from, and how do they morph from weirdos to killing machines?

"We're not entirely sure when and why that switch gets thrown," criminologist Michael Arntfield said.

The FBI estimates that less than one per cent of all murders in a given year are committed by serial killers, despite the oversized media footprint for these kinds of homicides.

According to the FBI's Behavioral Science Unit, "there is no single identifiable cause or factor that leads to the development of a serial killer. Rather, there are a multitude of factors that contribute to their development. The most significant factor is the serial killer's personal decision in choosing to pursue their crimes."

Peter Vronsky added: "It's a cocktail of things, it's never one thing. That's why I think it's even too early to write off old-fashioned Biblical evil, whatever that might be."

5

The Visalia Ransacker

What pushes prowlers, peepers and rapists to graduate to murder and sometimes multiple murders?

Often, several signs tell us which way the wind is blowing. Cruelty to pets and other animals, bed-wetting, and abuse are among the top markers.

No one knows for sure exactly what sent Joseph DeAngelo over the threshold to multiple rapes and homicides. Because he pleaded guilty to his heinous crimes, there was no trial. No psychiatric reports. Just the meat and potatoes of a rampage.

"Well, you know, it's really theories 'cause he's never talked. He's never told us exactly why he was doing these crimes," investigator Paul Holes told NPR.

"But he is the textbook example of the evolution of a serial killer. Different killers evolve different ways. But with DeAngelo, he started out as a Peeping Tom, standing outside, looking in windows. He was committing burglaries. Then he starts committing fetish burglaries when nobody's home."

Holes added, "After that, he progresses. He evolves into a serial rapist. He's now breaking into houses and attacking women and then ultimately couples. When he loses his law enforcement job – and you have to remember, he went to school. He got his criminal justice degree. He worked as a Roseville PD intern. He gets hired down in Exeter PD down in Southern – or middle California, Central California. He loses the thing that gave him that power and authority.

"What does he do? He goes down to Southern California, and he starts killing. So now the loss of that power and authority as a law enforcement officer basically pushed him over the brink from being a serial rapist to a serial killer."

And that's just one of the theories about DeAngelo's evolution from peeper to serial killer. There are countless others.

***

Exeter, California, is around 220 miles (354 km) south of the state capital, Sacramento. It's a tiny place, just 10,000 people, and sits in the fertile San Joaquin Valley near the foothills of the Sierra Nevada in Tulare County.

The area has a treasure trove of natural wonders, including the Sequoia National Park with its gigantic, majestic sequoia trees, notably the General Sherman Tree dominating the Giant Forest. In the summer, the temperatures soar with a July average of around 98°F (37°C).

Joseph DeAngelo attended Sacramento State University, where he earned his bachelor's degree in criminal justice. Determined to become a cop, he would do anything to make that a reality and took additional postgraduate courses, preparing himself for a career in law enforcement.

Following university, DeAngelo did a 32-week police internship with the local Roseville Police. That would set the stage for his future endeavours.

His fitness reports must have been sufficient because DeAngelo was hired by the Exeter Police Department in May 1973, where he would eventually become a burglary unit officer.

In some ways, Exeter was something of a homecoming for DeAngelo. Both his sisters, his mother and her second husband lived in Tulare County, where Exeter was located.

The small police force had just ten officers, so it was a wonderful hands-on experience for the aspiring crime fighter.

During the summer of 1974, a burglar began operating in nearby Visalia, and he had some odd kinks. At first, he hit houses on the suburban outskirts near the College of the Sequoias. Bedrooms were ransacked, and the contents of dresser drawers were dumped onto the floor. But little was taken, and the incidents were not big scores.

Instead, the villain, who would be known as the Visalia Ransacker, made off with single earrings, wedding bands, piggy banks, stamps and, occasionally, a handgun. One weekend, 13 separate homes were hit. Most noticeable was the women's underwear and lingerie scattered around the bedrooms.

In one episode, the women's undergarments were left inside-out. It seemed as if the Ransacker had given the underwear a test drive. Cops determined that when the mood suited, the Ransacker took the time to masturbate in these strangers' homes.

Sometimes he left the lingerie piled on the bed. In others, he taunted cops with the removed window screen prominently displayed on the bed. "This is how I got in," the fiend seemed to boast. The Visalia Ransacker was careful and clever.

There were the perfume bottles balanced on doorknobs to sound the alarm if someone entered the home and was about to catch him in the act. Once inside, the Ransacker opened doors and windows, allowing him an easy exit if he was caught.

One thing cops did have was a description of the prowler. Sort of. Sometimes they said he was tall; on other occasions witnesses said he was short. Neighbours told Visalia cops that the suspect had a round face; he was heavy but agile enough to leap a fence using one hand. It was murky and very helpful to the perpetrator. Investigators tracked the creeper from one burglarized house to the next.

There were fingerprints at the crime scenes, but detectives drew zeroes looking for a match. DeAngelo did not have a police record. No record. No prints.

By the time he became a cop, DeAngelo had ditched the James Dean vibe. Instead, he now looked like what he was – a small-town cop straight out of central casting. He was clean-cut and clean-shaven but had become beefier, sporting a fire hydrant-like neck.

What police in Visalia didn't know was that police in Rancho Cordova, on Sacramento's east side, had been dealing with an equally determined prowler. In a macabre twist, this suspect killed dogs.

In February 1972, an old hound named Pups became one of the first reported victims of what for a time became known as the Cordova Cat Burglar. Something of a local celebrity, Pups was a gentle, ten-year-old dog who was a bit overweight. Kids in the neighbourhood loved him.

The old hound was friendly, but he was loud.

Police believed that Pups' barking irked a prowler attempting to break into the house next door. The heartless suspect reached over a fence with a piece of wood and began battering the canine. His ribs were cracked, teeth knocked out, and his jaw was broken.

The community newspaper picked up on the sordid attack. The *Grapevine* also reported that there had been other killings of dogs in the rash of break-ins in Rancho Cordova. One victim told investigators that her dogs had been shot to death in the backyard. And with a twisted flourish, the animals were left in the woman's living room to bleed out.

Rancho Cordova was a new community, filled with mostly tract homes (multiple similar houses built on one tract of land). Most of the residents were military families stationed at the Mather Air Force Base. Others toiled for the defence contractors moving operations into the area. Most of its residents were young and just getting started.

After Pups the hound was killed, a new tenant who moved into the vacant home behind the property where the dog met its demise discovered a pathway he believed was used by the intruder for quick entries and exits. The man nailed his gate shut. When he got up the next day, the gate was open. His efforts had been shattered by what appeared to be a kick.

During the first six months of 1973, more than 50 homes had been entered. The burglar's modus operandi was to ignore high-value items that could bring real money from pawn shops, and instead, he concentrated on trinkets and other useless items.

"He took silver coins … he took cash, he took jewellery. Sometimes he'd take one set. One piece from the set," Sergeant Richard Shelby would later tell the *Los Angeles Times*, adding that the cops initially believed the break-ins were the work of kids.

One night, sitting in his radio car, he checked out a "suspicious circumstances" call in Rancho Cordova from dispatch. When he arrived at the scene, a couple told him they had reported a prowler lurking about a neighbour's home. But the house was locked, and nothing seemed unusual on the quiet street.

The scene was cleared, and officers were on their way for only a few minutes. Once again, the couple called the cops. They said they saw a man jump off the neighbour's roof and hit the ground running before vaulting over a fence.

Returning to the scene, Shelby scoured the property. At the door of the neighbour's garage, he made a foreboding discovery: a blood-soaked slab of firewood. Flesh was embedded into the grain. Shelby entered the home, shrouded in darkness, by himself. Nothing appeared amiss.

But halfway under one of the beds, he spotted the family's small dog. The pet had been disembowelled by vicious blows from a log. A burglar was unnerving enough. But the dog killings? This was something else. Still, police treated the events as minor, if not troubling, incidents.

Still, there was a creep factor that could not be dismissed.

One woman was awakened by the intruder when he touched her breast. In many instances, there was a break-in reported, but nothing had been stolen. The suspect did seem to enjoy pulling out women's underwear for all to see.

***

During the 1970s, police plied their trade without computers, databases, modern forensics and DNA testing. Multi-jurisdictional criminals and a lack of cooperation between law enforcement also hindered their crime-fighting efforts.

It's unlikely any investigator connected the Cordova Cat Burglar to the Visalia Ransacker – or even suspected they were the same man. But the Ransacker was about to graduate to murder.

On 11 September 1975, the elusive suspect entered a home on Whitney Lane. Beth Snelling, 16, awoke with a heavy man on top of her in her bed. The intruder wore a ski mask. Beth later told investigators that he had "mean eyes" and short, stubby fingers.

He put his hand over her mouth and nose. She couldn't breathe. In a low, rough whisper, the masked burglar snarled, "You're coming with me. Don't scream or I'll stab you."

The previous February, another peeper had been caught lurking outside Beth's bedroom window.

The home was owned by Claude Snelling, 45, a journalism professor at the College of the Sequoias. Snelling was awakened around 2 a.m. by strange sounds. He sprinted through the open back door and found himself facing a man wearing a ski mask in his carport. The suspect was attempting to kidnap his daughter, Beth.

The suspect fired twice, hitting Snelling and spinning him around. The stricken academic managed to get inside his home, where he collapsed. He died later in the hospital.

Now, the shooter punched and kicked the frightened Beth Snelling before dumping her on the ground and fleeing the scene. Later, a stolen bike was discovered nearby, and it was quickly linked to the killer.

Investigators tried numerous approaches, including hypnosis, to squeeze more details about the killer's identity. Police became more vigilant and offered a $4,000 reward for information leading to the arrest of the Visalia Ransacker. Still, the suspect did not slow down, and the ransackings continued.

Eerily, one month before the murder, Beth told cops she joked with her boyfriend about the Peeping Tom. Her boyfriend chuckled. They would almost assuredly hear him, the boyfriend told Beth. But when she got up, she jerked the curtain aside. And there he was.

The prowler had surprise written all over his face. Beth screamed, and she and her boyfriend ran out to give chase, but he had once again vanished into the ether.

So far, the Ransacker had struck at least 85 times in 15 months. And now, he had upped the ante to homicide.

Cops later determined that the gun used in the murder had been stolen from the scene of another burglary 11 days earlier, where again the Ransacker added a nice touch: the owner's underwear was strewn down the hallway of the home.

Then, the incidents seemed to inexplicably subside in Visalia. But that wasn't the case in Rancho Cordova, more than 200 miles (320 km) to the north.

The Cordova Cat Burglar hit four times in one night. The homes were on the same block and not coincidentally on a block where DeAngelo had once lived. Cops found one of the victims' purses in the shrubbery outside the home. That was once more small potatoes.

More concerning for the police was that the burglar's level of violence was increasing.

Three days after discovering the purse, a mother and her two daughters, aged 18 and 7, were sexually assaulted by the prowler. It wasn't far from where officers had found the disembowelled dog the year before.

According to the victims, the rapist was wearing a face covering not unlike a surgeon's mask. The attacker grabbed the mother and dragged her into a room with her older daughter. He tied them up and raped them repeatedly.

In a particularly cruel twist, the perpetrator also sexually assaulted the little girl. And as per his MO, he ransacked the house.

The Ransacker said little except to quietly snarl, "Shut up!" if they made a peep. His loot from this caper was just two jade rings. But the violent double rape had not previously been part of the Ransacker's twisted repertoire.

It was isolated, out of the ordinary. And it would take investigators nearly 50 years to connect the dots from the double rape to the mutilated dogs, 50-plus break-ins, the whopping 125 fetish burglaries and the murder in Visalia.

The death of Claude Snelling brought only a brief pause in the Ransacker's prowlings.

Visalia detectives were desperate to arrest the Ransacker, who was terrifying the citizens of the small California city.

To their credit, they used every method available at the time. They made maps of the homes where he had broken in. His footprints were tracked from house to house. And they tried to make sense of the killer's methodology.

And in December of 1975, they nearly got him.

Cops followed his shoe tracks from one home that had been ransacked. The prints led to other homes that revealed someone had been looking into windows and attempting to pry open doors. Investigators discovered that a Peeping Tom was peering into the bedroom of a 19-year-old woman. So the parents were told to rake the dirt beneath her window to see if the prowler returned. Right on time, the footprints reappeared.

One officer staked out the home, and the Ransacker returned.

Around 8:30 p.m. on 12 December 1975, the cop confronted the prowler who "screeched and acted panicky". Detective William McGowen fired his gun in warning. The prowler then pocketed his mask, drew his gun and squeezed the trigger. The bullet blew out the flashlight, barely missing McGowen's face.

Officers nearby rushed to help McGowen, but once again, the Ransacker slipped into the darkness, leaving as evidence the flashlight, a set of tennis shoe tracks, and Blue Chip Stamps and a sock filled with coins dropped by the suspect.

Forty break-ins later, in February 1976, cops met with criminal psychiatrist Dr Joel Fort. The headshrinker had a high profile and was an expert witness in the Patty Hearst kidnapping case.

But the Visalia Ransacker was not a low-rent hippie revolutionary.

Fort had also conducted numerous interviews with the notorious cult leader Charles Manson, whose so-called Family had butchered at least nine people in a frenzy of bloodlust in 1969. The Family was also suspected of an additional three murders.

From Fort's perspective, the news in Visalia was bad. The Ransacker had probably broken into hundreds more homes. And there was likely a lot more peeping as well, as he scoped out future capers.

Theft was not what drove him, Fort told detectives. Instead, the Ransacker was zeroed in on prowling and nurturing his voyeuristic fetish. His kick was "seeing people's intimate possessions".

"The suspect may very well enjoy the high risk or danger of the whole matter," Ford said. "The primary motivation for the crime is sexual."

Fort convinced the detectives that the psycho-sexual motivation needed to be explored further.

Next stop for cops was the Atascadero State Hospital in San Luis Obispo County on the Pacific coast. The secure facility contained an inordinate number of mentally ill sex offenders. Investigators spoke to psychiatrists and psychologists who worked with the deviants.

The doctors at Atascadero came to the same conclusion as Dr Fort. Noting that voyeurs typically have a geographic hunting zone no more than 15–20 minutes from where they live, the doctors suggested cops look further afield for their culprit. Within that time range, the Ransacker could be in Exeter.

And as with Fort, the doctors gave cops a stark warning: "The suspect can't quit."

And they explained the term paraphilia to investigators. The affliction in its mildest form is a penchant for some sort of kinky sex. At worst, it is a dark form of sexual perversion that can end in violent death.

Often it manifests itself in Peeping Toms and panty sniffers. More rarely, it's the gasoline that twists mere perverts into serial killers and criminal lunatics of all stripes.

Burglary is secondary or a cover. Sexual gratification is the driver.

More often than not, the prowler doesn't stop at peeping and begins ramping up the thrill factor. Research suggests that there are strong links between a serial fetish burglar and sexual homicide.

A 1999 clinical study revealed the intense connection between paraphilia and sexual murder. Eight out of ten women raped and murdered by a stranger in the safety of their home were slain by sexual burglars.

According to the *Los Angeles Times*, the smorgasbord of burglars, including voyeurs and fetish freaks, who started as peepers covers a pantheon of some of history's most violent serial killers.

The Boston Strangler, Albert DeSalvo; the Night Stalker, Richard Ramirez; the Gainesville Ripper, Danny Rolling; and the BTK Strangler, Dennis Rader, fill only a couple of lines in the roster.

Colonel Russell Williams was once Queen Elizabeth's pilot and later head of Canada's largest air force base. Williams had a thing for women's underwear and broke into more than 80 homes in his quest to satiate his bizarre desires. By the time he was finally arrested, Williams had raped four women and strangled two of them to death.

Like Russell Williams, Dennis Rader and a lot of his brethren in perversion, Joseph DeAngelo appeared outwardly normal.

Torn inside by their evil desires, these killers have spent their lives fighting the duality that resided within their souls. And then their sinister sides would declare their presence and manifest themselves in murder.

Their ability to commit so many crimes without capture was partly the result of the limited forensic tools available to police. But it also helped that a lifelong need to disguise abnormal sexual drives made them practised at deception.

Outwardly, they may have appeared normal, but beneath an often respectable veneer, demons roiled their troubled souls.

The close call with Detective William McGowen in December 1975, when the Ransacker shot out the cop's flashlight during a peeping expedition, seemed to cool his jets – at least in the Visalia area. The Ransacker struck just three more times.

Maybe the heat was too much in the small town, but there could have also been another reason the Ransacker spurned Visalia.

Joseph DeAngelo was on the move. He left the tiny Exeter Police Department for another small department in Auburn, a community on the northern outskirts of Sacramento and about 250 miles (400 km) from Exeter.

Rancho Cordova was just 30 minutes away from Auburn. That community had been the scene of scores of break-ins and dog mutilations at the hands of the Cordova Cat Burglar, who was still at large. But no one was ready for the slaughter that would follow from one end of the state to the other.

Paul Holes told NPR in 2019 that he had long been certain that his suspect lived somewhere in or around the state capital.

"I really came to the conclusion that our offender is Sacramento-based, probably still living in the Sacramento area, which DeAngelo was," Holes said.

"And I also concluded that I am dealing with a sophisticated and intelligent offender. Turns out the offender, the Golden State Killer, was a former cop. He understood law enforcement tactics. He had been trained as an investigator for burglaries. So he had skill sets that were up and beyond the average person in order to be able to develop tactics and get away with these crimes."

In the wake of the Cordova Cat Burglar and the Visalia Ransacker, victims were deeply traumatized by what had happened to them. It wasn't merely the feeling of violation of personal space, the survivors had been touched by inexplicable, life-altering violence.

For Beth Snelling and her family, dark days lay ahead. The family was haunted by the murder of father Claude even as volunteers replaced the blood-soaked carpet. According to the *Los Angeles Times*, Beth and her brother slept with their mother in her king-size bed.

The fear never left.

6

The East Area Rapist

By 1973, there was a new woman caught in Joseph DeAngelo's sights.

She was law student Sharon Marie Huddle. The pair married in November 1973, with the ceremony held in Auburn, where he was now a police officer following his departure from the tiny Exeter Police Department.

His heart had been shattered when his classmate Bonnie Jean Colwell called off their engagement in 1971 after he became increasingly manipulative and abusive.

Asking her to help him cheat on an abnormal psychology test was the last straw. Following their split, DeAngelo even tried to drag Bonnie to Reno for a quickie wedding. The intervention of her father was the only thing that stopped his loopy scheme.

That was then. By all appearances, DeAngelo had discovered love again and seemed ready to move into a stable new phase of middle-class life.

The DeAngelos bought a house in Citrus Heights in suburban Sacramento. It was the same house where he was arrested decades later. Three daughters followed in quick succession as Sharon studied to become a lawyer before becoming a successful divorce attorney in 1982. It was a remarkable professional feat for a mother of three.

The majority of DeAngelo's crimes would be committed while he was married to Huddle and helping to raise their three children. None of them suspected there was anything amiss with the burly cop. One daughter later declared he was the "perfect father".

Their wedding announcement in *The Sacramento Bee* described DeAngelo as a graduate of Folsom High School and Sacramento State. The wedding was held at Auburn First Congregational Church.

When he joined the Exeter Police Department, the local newspaper announced his arrival and said the young cop "believes that without law and order there can be no government and without a democratic government, there can be no freedom. Law enforcement is his career, he says, and his job is serving the community."

The trials, tribulations and triumphs of Joseph DeAngelo's young family were not unlike those of his cohort, but the pair happily blended into their suburban paradise. If there were any fears or concerns about Joe, his wife didn't tell anyone. She would later say she never had a clue that by night, her husband transformed into one of his criminal guises.

But some reports suggested the pair began growing distant as early as the late 1970s before officially separating in 1991. Still, Huddle did not divorce DeAngelo until 2019, one year after he was arrested.

To this day, questions remain about how much Huddle may have known about DeAngelo's crimes and nocturnal activities. When he was finally arrested, she issued a terse statement to the media.

"My thoughts and prayers are for the victims and their families," Huddle said. "The press has relentlessly pursued interviews of me. I will not be giving any interviews for the foreseeable future. I ask the press to please respect my privacy and that of my children."

And that was it. In a murder investigation where both cops and the public were looking for any kind of insight into the serial killer, it would not be coming from his ex-wife, even though the pair had been married for 46 years. People who knew the couple said that far from being a monster, DeAngelo was a trustworthy, reliable man who was a devoted father. Whatever excuses he told his wife for his nocturnal absences seemed to pass muster.

He'd also been awarded numerous medals for his 22-month service in Vietnam, where he lost a finger. DeAngelo was an educated and respected authority figure. After all, he was a cop.

What Huddle didn't – and likely couldn't – know was that the murderous Visalia Ransacker and the Cordova Cat Burglar were the same person, if the busy mom even gave the criminality she read in the newspaper a thought. She was also no doubt unaware that detectives believed their suspect was, in all likelihood, a police officer.

"It was a lot more than a hunch," former Sacramento sheriff's deputy Wendell Phillips said. "There was no doubt he was either military or law enforcement or both."

And there was a new fiend on the loose. This time his tag was the East Area Rapist. By the time Huddle and DeAngelo became parents in the autumn of 1981, this new villain had committed 50 rapes.

Law enforcement in Sacramento had a litany of criminal headaches on their hands during the mid-1970s. Not only were they dealing with the East Area Rapist, there was also a fiend known as the Vampire of Sacramento.

His reign of terror lasted less than a month, but by the time it ended, six people were dead.

Richard Trenton Chase was born in Sacramento in 1950 and, from an early age, displayed evidence of a budding psychopath. He was also a hypochondriac who sometimes complained that someone had "stolen" his pulmonary artery.

By his teens, he had developed a taste for reefer, booze and LSD. Not exactly a recipe for clear-headed thinking. Sometimes he would walk around the apartment he shared with pals naked, even if company was visiting.

Chase also had a penchant for killing and disembowelling animals, which he would eat raw, sometimes mixed with Coca-Cola in a blender. Needless to say, he had several stays at California mental institutions.

As a result of his fixation on blood, orderlies called him "Dracula" after Bram Stoker's famed vampire. He was eventually released into the care of his mother, who weaned him off his pills and brought some stability back to his troubled life. It didn't last long.

On 29 December 1977, he shot to death engineer Ambrose Griffin in a drive-by while the father-of-two helped his wife bring groceries from their car. But that was merely a warm-up for Chase.

One of the bizarre things about Chase was that if a door was locked, he took it as a sign not to kill the inhabitants of homes. An unlocked door? An open invitation to kill.

The next victim was a young woman named Teresa Wallin who was three months pregnant. Chase shot Wallin to death on 23 January 1978. This time, Chase had sexual intercourse with her corpse as he stabbed her with a butcher's knife. And in a macabre twist, he removed her organs, cut off a nipple and drank her blood from a yogurt cup.

As a final indignity, he stuffed dog faeces down her throat. Her husband, David Wallin, recalled the horror of discovering her mutilated body. He told *The Sun* in 2021 that he began screaming and wailing.

"I had no idea where I was, or who or what I had seen," Wallin said. "It was just beyond all comprehension. All I know is the noise I was making; I was screaming and screaming so much that my neighbours raced over to help me."

He added: "It was just horrific. Walking into that spot and seeing what I saw, it was just beyond. I was just crying out, 'Why? Why? Why?' Whoever it was, why had they been so cruel to me? Why would they do this?"

Chase wasn't done. Four days later, he broke into the home of 38-year-old Evelyn Miroth and her friend Danny Meredith. He proceeded to murder Meredith with the Saturday night special .22-calibre handgun he carried. Miroth, her six-year-old son Jason and her 22-month-old nephew David Ferreira were next. Chase then mutilated Miroth and had sex with her corpse before cannibalizing her and drinking her blood.

He then fled in Meredith's car and took little David Ferreira's body with him after being interrupted by a knock on the door. His handprints were all over the place.

Five days later, the Vampire of Sacramento was arrested. When police raided his apartment, they discovered a blood-filled blender. He had also eaten parts of little David's brain and taken his body back to his apartment to cannibalize before ditching the body in a church parking lot.

At his 1979 trial, Chase's lawyers argued he was insane and the charges should be lowered to second-degree murder. California wanted him in the green room at San Quentin sucking gas. It took the jury just five hours to sentence Chase to die. Even the hardened killers on death row found Chase creepy beyond words, often urging him to kill himself.

In December 1980, he did just that, beating the executioner to the punch.

But the East Area Rapist was a slipperier beast. His horizons had also expanded. And investigators quickly ruled out any connection between the East Area Rapist and the Vampire of Sacramento.

And he was enjoying taunting the police. In December 1977, a person claiming to be the EAR sent a poem entitled

"Excitement's Crave" to *The Sacramento Bee*, the city mayor's office and local TV station KVIE.

Excitement's Crave

All those mortal's surviving birth
Upon facing maturity,
Take inventory of their worth
To prevailing society.

Choosing values becomes a task;
Oneself must seek satisfaction.
The selected route will unmask
Character when plans take action.

Accepting some work to perform
At fixed pay, but promise for more,
Is a recognized social norm,
As is decorum, seeking lore.

Achieving while others lifting
Should be cause for deserving fame.
Leisure tempts excitement seeking,
What's right and expected seems tame.

"Jessie James" has been seen by all,
And "Son of Sam" has an author.
Others now feel temptations call.
Sacramento should make an offer.

To make a movie of my life
That will pay for my planned exile.
Just now I'd like to add the wife
Of a Mafia lord to my file.

Your East Area Rapist
And deserving pest.
See you in the press or on T.V.

Further south, the maniac known as the Original Night Stalker would soon begin terrorizing Southern California.

Behind his facade of respectable middle-class propriety, trouble percolated just beneath Joseph DeAngelo's well-curated facade.

Law enforcement was the most important thing in DeAngelo's life. He thrived on the power a badge and a gun gave him. The beefy cop had aspired to a career in policing since he was a young boy. There was little that was more important to him.

But in 1979, it all came apart. DeAngelo was fired from the Auburn Police Department after he was caught stealing dog repellent and a hammer. Both items came in handy during his nocturnal adventures.

But no one put the pieces together at the time.

It was then-Police Chief Nick Willick who fired him. DeAngelo later filed a lawsuit against Willick and the police, but it went nowhere. DeAngelo took his sacking very personally.

"The investigator told me that Joseph had gone to my house one night to kill me, and said that he walked around the house looking in the windows but couldn't find my bedroom," Willick said.

"A short time after he had been fired, I woke up one morning. My 4-year-old daughter was laying alongside the bed. She said, 'Dad, last night there was someone looking in my bedroom window with a flashlight.'"

Willick added, "I just never saw him as a person who could, you know, kill somebody."

He later told *Good Morning America* that to this day he feels embarrassed that DeAngelo, in one of his murderous guises, was raping and murdering under the nose of police.

Around the time DeAngelo joined the Auburn Police, the first crime was committed by the East Area Rapist in the Sacramento area. By the time the monster stopped, 45 women had been raped.

"I just wish we, it could have, you know, been stopped a long time ago," Willick said.

The former police chief said not long after DeAngelo was hired, the future serial killer gave him a tour of his home. DeAngelo told Willick that he and his wife slept in separate bedrooms.

Willick told *Good Morning America* that he later wondered if that living arrangement may have enabled DeAngelo to slip out of his house in the middle of the night.

Investigator Paul Holes told NPR in 2019 that he found an old newspaper clipping regarding DeAngelo's time with the Auburn Police.

"And eventually, there's an article, a newspaper article, found where he had been fired from Auburn PD for shoplifting dog repellent and a hammer. And he had been fired by this chief of Auburn, this Nick Willick," Holes said.

"So I end up talking to Nick. And Nick, during that conversation, he doesn't know I'm looking at the East Area Rapist/Golden State Killer case.

"He talks about when DeAngelo was on admin leave during the termination process. Nick's at home asleep in his bed. And his daughter comes into his room and says, 'Dad, there's a man standing outside my bedroom window shining a flashlight into it.'"

Holes added, "And Nick says, 'Paul, I knew that was DeAngelo. I jumped up. I ran outside. I saw shoe impressions all around the perimeter of the back of my house. But I knew that was Joe.' And that's when the hairs on the back of my neck stood up because I go, 'That's exactly what the Golden State Killer was doing.'

"And it was really – that was really the turning point, where I'm going, OK, this Joseph DeAngelo, in addition to other aspects about him, that right there is where we need to get this guy's DNA and see if he is the Golden State Killer."

***

The first crime committed by the East Area Rapist occurred in mid-1976 in the Sacramento area. Soon, the city was terrorized.

On 18 June 1976, the East Area Rapist struck in a scene that was remarkably similar to the horrific attacks that would follow. A 23-year-old Rancho Cordova woman was startled to see a man in a blue T-shirt and white ski mask in her bedroom doorway. He wasn't wearing pants and his penis was erect. At first, the victim thought she was having a nightmare.

That notion was quickly dismissed when the prowler pounced on her bed. Pressing a knife blade into her right temple, he whispered, "If you make one move or sound, I'll stick this knife in you."

Once she was subdued and tied up with an electrical cord from her hair dryer, the man raped her. When he left, she dialled "0".

Sacramento's nightmare was in its infancy.

Detectives would encounter numerous scenes like the one over the next two years in Rancho Cordova and elsewhere in suburban Sacramento. Same MO almost every time, particularly victims who had been bound.

Would-be victims didn't know it, but the rapist would give them a heads-up. They would receive a hang-up call or crank call in the days and sometimes hours preceding the attack. And detectives noticed that there were odd scratches on the window screens. Were they code for which houses the rapist intended to invade?

Initial descriptions pegged the attacker as probably young (18 to 30), lean and athletic. He was able to jump over roofs and fences with little effort.

But to most of the victims, he was a sinister masked figure standing next to their bed and shining a flashlight in their eyes. He quietly snarled that all he wanted was food and money. Of course, those items were not what drove the rapist.

On 18 December 1976, 15-year-old Kris Pedretti was home alone while her parents attended a Christmas party. She would be his tenth victim. She was playing the piano when he suddenly emerged. He was wearing a red ski mask, telling the young woman all he wanted was money.

But the prowler put a knife to her throat to underscore the potential for violence. He whispered in the terrified teen's ear, "Do what I say or I'll kill you and be gone in the dark."

That phrase gained immortality and would serve as the title of author Michelle McNamara's seminal book on the investigation.

Next came the hands tied behind the back. In this instance, he tied her up with her sister's shoelaces that he had stolen earlier. And he made his victim masturbate him with hand lotion. This became one of the killer's rituals. Investigators came to understand that forced masturbation was one of their quarry's identifying traits.

Then he asked about her sexual history. For two agonizing hours, the maniac raped her three times. She told the rapist she was a virgin, but he raped her anyway.

"He alternated leaving me outside, naked in the winter cold, and bringing me in different rooms where he raped me," Pedretti later said.

With a knife held to her throat, the rapist asked until she answered in the affirmative, "Oh, isn't this good?"

She was left on a couch, blindfolded, bound, and gagged. But at least she was alive. Eventually, she got free of the bindings and called for help.

In addition to his gruesome handiwork, some victims told cops that before he struck, he appeared nervous and maybe a little frightened. Once the victims were bound, he was in total control.

"He seemed [at times] unable to have intercourse," Michelle McNamara wrote in *Los Angeles* magazine.

"There was a lot of fidgeting, getting up and leaving the room, then returning. He never put his full weight on his victims but draped their legs around him and rarely touched them. He liked to make them use crass words. Sometimes a blindfolded victim would be asked to identify what she was hearing."

He would ask as he masturbated: "What does it sound like?"

"One victim decided to try a bit of reverse psychology and told him he was a good lover," McNamara wrote. "He stopped abruptly and said no one had ever told him that before. People made fun of him because he was small [his penis], he said."

The rapist appeared to be following some sort of bizarre script he wanted his helpless victims to follow. And if the women or the situation went off script or if there was a delay, he would threaten to kill them.

"He might have been acting out a scene in his head, but for his victims, the terror was in not knowing how it was going to end," McNamara wrote.

It also appeared to police that the rapist enjoyed playing cat and mouse with cops. When the Sacramento Police said in the media that the East Area Rapist only targeted women and girls who were home alone, he changed tactics. He began attacking couples.

One man stood up at a community meeting and questioned how any men could fail to protect their wives. The man and his wife went into the files as case number 21. They too became victims. The husband had been subdued by the East Area Rapist, who proceeded to rape his wife.

On 2 February 1978, the Golden State Killer would commit his first double killing. The victims were a couple, a harbinger of future victimology. But there were some aspects of the murders that didn't fit his typical MO.

USAF Sergeant Brian Maggiore, 21, and his wife Katie, 20, normally walked their miniature grey poodle, a pup called Thumper, through their Rancho Cordova neighbourhood near the American River. The young couple were possibly oblivious to the ominous spectre of the East Area Rapist then terrorizing the city. He had already murdered once, and his rapes and break-ins were escalating.

Cops say that around 9 p.m., the couple and Thumper embarked on their nightly walk. About two blocks from their home, they encountered the rapist. The details remain murky. Was there some sort of confrontation? Was the incident targeted or random? Or did the couple witness something and decide to intervene?

One witness said that the East Area Rapist was chasing the couple through one yard and into another. The horrified witness watched as the prowler raised a handgun and fired at the fleeing couple.

Area residents heard gunshots along with breaking glass and chilling screams. The East Area Rapist jumped a gate, fell into some bushes, then hit the ground running.

Witnesses would later say he was wearing a ski mask and holding a pistol in his right hand. He was wearing a brown leather jacket and black shoes. Others in the area said they had seen a man matching that description.

In the backyard of 10165 La Alegria Drive, high school sweethearts Brian and Katie were discovered shot to death. Their dog was in a backyard swimming pool.

Cops long suspected that the double slaying was connected to the East Area Rapist. Several sexual assaults had been committed by the East Area Rapist in the Cordova Meadows neighbourhood. And the killer left a pre-tied shoelace behind that matched the rapist's knots.

Experts remain puzzled whether the rapist's bloodlust was at fever pitch that night or whether the Maggiores were eliminated to cover his tracks. Most likely the East Area Rapist was prowling, looking for a victim when he encountered the couple.

***

Sacramento became paralyzed with fear. Store shelves were cleared of guns, locks, alarms and other security enhancers. One family tied tambourines to their doors and windows and called the atmosphere "crazy with fear".

And as often happens in red ball investigations (high-profile cases attracting media attention), the public wanted to help. Most tips were useless, though, and only muddied the investigation and bogged down detectives. By turns, the rapist drove a Chevy station wagon, a Volkswagen or a Ford Mustang. The car was loud or it was quiet. Its colour was light. Or it was dark.

The physical description of the East Area Rapist also varied, depending on who you talked to. He was slim. He was stocky. He was tall. He was shorter. He carried two revolvers. He came unarmed. He had tattoos, or maybe he didn't. One ten-year-old boy whose mother was raped said the attacker had "very white skin and very blue eyes" and maybe a funny, bow-legged walk.

While the East Area Rapist/Golden State Killer was proving to be a clever, elusive criminal, it wasn't all smooth sailing.

One man, who described himself as a light sleeper, awoke in the early morning hours of 6 July 1979 to see a prowler just a few feet from his bed donning a ski mask. Instinctively, the man jumped out of bed.

He said, "What the fuck are you doing here?"

The man did not look like an arch-criminal. He was wearing a dark blue ski mask but with comical, half-assed homemade eyeholes cut out. And then the man got in the intruder's face and locked eyes with him. His brazenness appeared to stun the prowler.

The suspect just blinked and stepped back. But something in the man and his wife recognized or sensed who they were dealing with, and they fled their home. Later, under hypnosis with detectives, the man noted that the intruder's eyes were deep set, almost boyish. He had large irises and lush eyelashes.

***

After being fired from his job as a police officer, DeAngelo was hired as a truck mechanic for the Save Mart grocery store chain. He would work there for 27 years without incident.

"He was a mechanic," said a Save Mart company spokeswoman. "None of his actions in the workplace would have led us to suspect any connection to crimes being attributed to him."

Even as the Golden State Killer began his murderous frenzy, the crimes were spread over a wide geographic area. No one had connected the dots that, rather than many monsters, detectives were, in fact, chasing just one man.

If Huddle knew or suspected any nefarious doings by her husband, she didn't let on. However, as the marriage began crumbling, she purchased a second house in Roseville.

Still, they stayed largely under one roof, albeit in separate bedrooms, and shared parenting without issue.

One of their three daughters would become an emergency room physician. Another was a graduate student at the University of California in Davis. The third daughter and Sharon Huddle's granddaughter were living with DeAngelo when he was arrested.

Huddle divorced her husband one year after his 2018 arrest. It is not clear whether she was in shock or disbelief. Nonetheless, the length of time it took to formally divorce Joseph DeAngelo after 45 years raised some eyebrows.

"The DA's office can subpoena her," said attorney Mark Reichel, adding that dissolving the marriage union rids Huddle of previous legal rights. "She loses her right to say no. She can't talk about communications, but she can talk about observations. 'He wasn't home this night. This night he came home with these clothes.'"

But what Huddle could also possibly provide was insight into her former husband's mind. His quirks, passions, loves and hatreds.

Reichel added, "She can really be a domestic diary of the daily activities of this person."

After DeAngelo pleaded guilty, Huddle painted herself as a victim of his horrific reign of terror as well. She claimed he lied to her about his comings and goings, particularly when she worked the late shift at a fast food joint. She insisted she was in the dark.

Acknowledging that the family did not experience his violence directly, once given the disinfectant of light, Huddle said the revelations had a "devastating and pervasive effect".

"I will never be the same person," Huddle wrote in a victim impact statement. "I now live every day with the knowledge of how he attacked and severely damaged hundreds of innocent people's lives and murdered 13 innocent people who were loved and have now been missed for 40 years or more.

"I live every day with post-traumatic distress where any unexpected noise, or movement of any person or object, can be perceived by my mind as a threat to me. Simple everyday experiences, such as a car moving from one lane into another lane behind your car, can bring fear to me."

Banal tasks like grocery shopping had also become a source of terror.

"Once while shopping at Trader Joe's grocery store, a hand touched my forearm while I was looking into a freezer," she wrote.

"My heart began to race, and my body jolted. I was terrified that I was about to be harmed, when in reality, someone I knew just wanted to say hello to me.

"I have lost my ability to trust people. I trusted the defendant when he told me he had to work, or was going pheasant hunting, or going to visit his parents hundreds of miles away."

Huddle added: "When I was not around, I trusted he was doing what he told me he was doing. Now, without the ability to trust, my relationships with other people are severely impacted."

Still, there was something or someone that Huddle failed to mention in her statement.

Joseph James DeAngelo Jr. She did not utter his name.

Not once.

7

The Mind of a Killer

California cops would soon be duelling with a serial killer operating hundreds of miles away from his typical hunting grounds. Sex was clearly the driving factor, but the killer was careful, elusive, ruthless and not prone to making mistakes.

The multiple jurisdictions thwarted an identification and arrest. There were no databases and little inter-departmental cooperation.

Detectives tried to unravel the psychology behind the Golden State Killer, but answers were slim. Only theories, some good, some bad, offered any insight into the workings of his mind.

Dr Michael Arntfield of Western University is one of the world's foremost experts on serial killers and cold cases. In several interviews conducted as research for this book, Arntfield admits that because there was never a trial and, as a result, no psychiatric reports, the Golden State Killer is an outlier.

A terrifying enigma.

"So he exists in a blind spot in history in terms of forensic psychology, and therefore I am reluctant to use the term profile," Arntfield said.

He added that until Michelle McNamara, author of *I'll Be Gone in the Dark*, coined the moniker "Golden State Killer", the crimes remained in relative obscurity, because by the time investigators linked the two separate sets of crimes of the East Area Rapist and the Original Night Stalker and created the awkward portmanteau EARONS, hardly anyone was familiar with either.

Arntfield noted that the lack of a "cultural footprint" kept the widespread crimes comparatively on the down-low outside the Sacramento area. And with so many serial killers operating in Southern California, the so-called Original Night Stalker murders slipped into the abyss.

"For years, I had an assignment on a final exam in a course that I offered. I would provide his writings. One of them was a map that he drew," he said.

"I mean, he was a prolific writer as part of his 'homework'. There was like a compendium of notes left near one of the murder scenes, and it contained weird ramblings and a map of where his victims' houses were or where his latest victim's house was.

"I assumed basically based on this and what you know about house offenders – serial offenders see themselves as literary characters. This is in my book, *Murder in Plain English*."

Part of a serial killer's ethos and drive to kill is focused on how they perceive themselves and the way they make their way through the world.

Arntfield explained that there are "four literary archetypes" serial killers adhere to.

"They've read things, they've seen things, they understand, they have the self-awareness to see themselves as characters in a story, which is why so many of them feel compelled to write stories about their crimes and thoughts," Arntfield added.

"And this ranges from people like the Son of Sam, who are actually engaging in correspondence, to Charles Ng and Leonard Lake."

Son of Sam – David Berkowitz – terrorized the outer boroughs of New York City in the late 1970s. During his homicidal rampage, he wrote bizarre letters to famed *New York Daily News* columnist Jimmy Breslin and columnist Steve Dunleavy at the *New York Post*.

Survivalist serial killers Ng and Lake lived in a lurid fantasy world in the depths of the California wilderness, where they would kidnap women, keep them as sex slaves, and rape and torture them before they were murdered.

More recently, South Carolina murderer Todd Kohlhepp took his literary skills a step further. Between 2003 and 2016, he murdered seven people. In addition, he kidnapped and raped at least two women.

Alarmingly, Kohlhepp told cops he killed many more. And they believe him.

Following his kills, Kohlhepp would bizarrely post reviews of the weapons and products he used on Amazon.com. Investigators in Spartanburg County discovered a slew of darkly humorous product reviews for the sorts of tools a serial killer would need: padlocks, shovels, tasers, and gun accessories. He signed his reviews "Me".

Kohlhepp kept his prisoners in shipping containers, and in one missive, he raved about a brand of padlocks: "solid locks.. have 5 on a shipping container.. wont stop them.. but sure will slow them down til they are too old to care." *[sic]*

One review for a portable shovel read: "keep in car for when you have to hide the bodies and you left the full size shovel at home…. does not come with a midget, which would have been nice."

On his Amazon.com wish list, Kohlhepp used his name.

On 26 May 2017, Kohlhepp pleaded guilty to seven counts of murder, two counts of kidnapping, and one count of criminal sexual assault and was sentenced to seven consecutive life sentences without the possibility of parole in a plea bargain.

If he had gone to trial, Kohlhepp would have been a prime candidate for the death penalty.

When his mother later asked him how many people he had murdered, Kohlhepp cooly replied: "You do not have enough fingers."

While investigating the East Area Rapist's 42nd attack in Danville, detectives found three sheets of notebook paper close to where a suspicious vehicle had reportedly been parked. Officers believed that the pages had been dropped accidentally; perhaps they dropped out of a bag.

One sheet appeared to be a homework essay describing the heroics of US 7th Cavalry General George Armstrong Custer, who, along with 200 of his men, was slaughtered at the Battle of Little Bighorn in 1876.

A second sheet contains a journal-like entry describing a teacher who made students write lines. Whoever the author, almost certainly DeAngelo, they bitterly complained using poor spelling and grammar about the line writing, describing the shame and anger that it caused:

Mad is the word, the word that reminds me of 6th grade. I hated that year … I wish I had know what was going to be going on during my 6th-grade year, the last and worst year of elementary school. Mad is the word that remains in my head about my dreadful year as a 6th grader. My Madness was one that was caused by disapointments that hurt me very much. Dissapointments from my teacher, such as feild trips that were planed, then canncled. My 6th-grade teacher gave me a lot of dissapointments which made me very mad and made me built a state of haterd in my heart, no one ever let me down that hard before and I never hated anyone as much as I did him. Disapointment wasn't the only reason that made me mad in my sixth-grade class, another was getting in trouble at school espeically talking thats what really bugged me was writing sentences, those awful sentence that my teacher made … me write, hours and hours Id sit and write 50-100-150 sentence day and night I write those dreadful Paragraphs which embarrased me and more inportant it made me ashamed of myself which in turn, deep down in side made me realize that writing sentence wasn't fair it wasn't fair to make me suffer like that, it just wasn't fair to make me sit and wright until my bones aked, until my hand felt every horrid pain it ever had and as I wrote, I got mader and mader until I cried, I cried because I was ashamed I cried because I was discusted, I cried because I was mad, and I cried for myself, kid who kept on having to write those dane sentences. My Angryness from Sixth grade will scar my memory for life and I will be ashamed for my sixth grade year forcver.

On the final sheet the attacker is believed to have left behind was a hand-drawn map of what appeared to be a suburban neighbourhood, with the word "punishment" scrawled across the reverse side.

Investigators were unable to identify the area depicted in the map, although the artist had some knowledge of architectural layout and landscape design.

Retired Detective Larry Pool posited that the map was a work of fiction, a fantasy location representing the rapist's perfect striking ground.

"There's a literary compulsion, so these people are very much aware of how they fit into stories," Michael Arntfield said, adding that normal people also have private narratives.

The criminologist said every serial killer fits into one of the four archetypes. DeAngelo is what Arntfield calls the "adventurer".

"The idea being your average person, yeah, what they do has a focus, it has a high school feel to it. 'If I had a story on Hallmark, like a Hallmark Channel, my high school would be like this, and this would be the plot, this would be the theme. College, it looks like this. My early working life, it looks like this,'" he said.

Most people's fantasies are normal or, as Arntfield said, "reasonably accurate or authentic". But the majority of serial killers live in their heads, where fantasy runs rife.

"Unless you're dealing with an extreme narcissist, you know, in hindsight, you know they were the target of a conspiracy because everyone was threatened by them or something like that," he said.

"Whereas a serial offender, because they've existed … they're already grappling with so many subsidiary sexual personality disorders. Again, like I said, one of these four is typically very entrenched in the stream and gives them inauthentic impressions of themselves.

"So, which one is DeAngelo? I see him as the hero, the tragedy and the adventure."

Another archetype, Arntfield said, is the revenge-driven character.

"That would be more like the incel type. With DeAngelo, it's the adventurer or something similar, but someone who sees murder as a quest, essentially," he said.

"Which explains the elaborate planning, the elaborate stories, the experimental departures from it, where he's committing animal mutilations and conducting serial rapes and conducting serial murders simultaneously."

As detectives began investigating DeAngelo, they eventually linked him to earlier crimes. Some investigators had suspected for years that there were many more crimes at hand than the ones linked to their specific geographic boundaries.

"This is all conjecture, but they looked at the Visalia Ransacker. There were a series of animal kidnappings and mutilations that were sitting there unsolved," Arntfield said. "They were contemporaneous with the ransacking. This would not be an uncommon first set of crimes for a serial killer."

What's the payoff for the ransacker, rapist or Golden State Killer? One of our most primal emotions is Joseph DeAngelo's catnip.

"This is someone who draws great sexual and emotional satisfaction from the fear of suffering or humiliation of others, and that exists along a massive spectrum," Arntfield said.

"I mean, you could have a sadistic boss who just loves needling people, or you could have somebody who actually could only sexually climax through acts like watching or doing someone being strangled to death. And they're looking at them."

Creating such a terrifying creature as Joseph DeAngelo is not an easy task. Many aspects of their lives have to fall into sync to result in serial murder.

One card in the deck is the absence of parents. One of the most common traits of a serial killer. For DeAngelo, his Air Force officer father was often away on assignment. His mother toiled long hours at a greasy spoon, leaving the future Golden State Killer as essentially the family babysitter and maid.

He cared for his siblings, got them to school and back home, did the laundry and cooked the family meals.

"Some common traits of serial killers involve an absent parent," Arntfield said.

"And there's no way to quantify, okay, this one outranks that, but again, these traits aren't positive, but they're co-related. So if you have a parent who's an alcoholic, you're not necessarily gonna be a serial killer."

One trait doesn't necessarily turn someone into a homicidal maniac, but the more traits that are present, the greater the propensity for violence.

"When you start adding these things up … a lot of these guys have things in common: unstable addresses, frequent moving. That could be as a result of housing insecurity, or it could be a result of being a military brat."

He added, "An absent parent, an abusive parent, or both and some kind of substance abuse, typically in the house, which is correlated with the neglect and the abuse. Most of these parents aren't teetotalers."

One aspect of DeAngelo's life that caught Arntfield's attention was his place of residence. He moved into the quiet Citrus Heights neighbourhood and never moved despite his murderous travels.

In fact, he was still living in the suburban abode when cops swooped in decades later.

"The first thing that occurred to me is that this guy never moved," Arntfield said. "Because that's always the theory. This guy's gone dormant for 40 years; we've got his DNA, but there's been no resurfacing, like he must reside somewhere like that."

The last known murder committed by the Golden State Killer was that of Janelle Cruz on Sunday, 4 May 1986, in Irvine in Orange County, south of Los Angeles. For the killer, it was a 424-mile (682 km) quest from his home base.

"So, 30 years ago, this guy goes on a rampage, and then he stops. That's what I would love to know, so there are a couple of cases of guys [serial killers] aging out. They are physically unable to commit their crimes of choice anymore," Arntfield said.

Because of technological advances, many killers who terrorized communities in the 1970s are, like DeAngelo, finally being captured. Most are elderly and have not killed in years.

Serial murder is typically, with few exceptions, a young man's game. Either they are physically incapable of committing homicide on a wide scale, or the circumstances in their lives change.

Virtually no one begins their murderous journey in their late fifties or early sixties.

One exception was Kevin Gavin.

Gavin, 66, ingratiated himself with the three elderly female tenants of his Brooklyn apartment building. He ran their errands and did favours for the trio, and the women let him into their apartments. As he built trust, the women had no idea they were dealing with a predator.

Myrtle McKinney, 82, was the first to die. She was stabbed to death in November 2015 and left on her kitchen floor. Jacolia James, 83, was next. She was found with suspicious injuries to her head and neck on 30 April 2019. The final known victim was Juanita Caballero, 78, whose family discovered her on the floor with a telephone cord wrapped around her neck in January 2021.

Detectives speculated that the women owed Gavin money. His criminal record was strictly low rent: drug use, burglary and a half-cocked insurance scam.

But most elderly serial killers are brought into court in wheelchairs and attached to oxygen tanks.

"By the time DeAngelo showed up in court, he was in a wheelchair and whatever," the criminologist said. "But their [the police] first glimpse of him, he's moving a fridge by himself out of his house. I mean, he was just like one of these old, barrel-chested men, like he could still probably kill people."

Others, like BTK ("bind, torture, kill") Strangler Dennis Rader, found being a serial killer and a pillar of the community at the same time simply too much to handle.

Between 1974 and 1991, Rader terrorized Wichita, Kansas, with a slew of sex murders. He racked up at least ten victims and probably more. But he also took a six-year break during his orgy of death.

"Dennis Rader, he said that actually the double life he was leading became unsustainable and he knew he was going to eventually make mistakes and get caught," Arntfield said.

"So he focused on being a father and blending in. He would have preferred to have kept killing, but the banality of being a suburban father in Park City, Kansas, got in the way of his hobby."

"He's very candid about it. And again, we have admissions from him. He's very clear in court. He says, 'I had an outfit.' He's a classic adventurer and had a full outfit that he wore; he planned it elaborately."

Again, Rader was very literary. Like a novelist plotting his characters, locales and the hero's journey, Rader doubled down on the adventurer serial killer archetype.

"Rader planned murders the way people would plan to climb a certain mountain. What am I gonna wear? What am I gonna eat beforehand? How am I gonna control my breathing? What time of day am I gonna leave?"

Joseph DeAngelo was different.

"We have none of that with DeAngelo, so we have to look at what common characteristics he shares with other similar statistically multifaceted serial sexual murderers who commit home invasions," Arntfield added.

With DeAngelo, we know from family members and friends that his mother was overbearing and his father, allegedly an alcoholic, was absent and abusive to young Joe. And because he was a military brat, the family moved around.

As a young man, DeAngelo may have felt helpless in a rapidly changing world. But there was one profession that offered him clarity, power and authority.

That was becoming a police officer, his chosen career path.

"For the power, absolutely, he becomes a cop, and that was what a number of my students noticed, and what I noticed is the use of the flashlight," Arntfield said.

"All the victims talked about this flashlight, not like this is how someone can rob you. You instead have the tactical use of the flashlight to instil fear, power and authority.

"So to grab it, like it's close to your body, you can't move. And the fact that he's able to vault a fence. In one case, and this is in *I'll Be Gone in the Dark*, he's able to vault a fence and as a neighbour is chasing him, he basically takes a shot at his back that goes off the guy's belt."

The shot is a tough one to make, but it indicates clearly that the man firing the gun is proficient with firearms, even in the dark. His aim wasn't like a gangbanger with his first Glock; it was deadly accurate.

When police swarmed the area, it suggested that he understood police deployment and containment techniques.

Arntfield added, "We talked about that frequently, but it was clear this person had military or law enforcement training or was aware of law enforcement operations."

A serial rapist who fits the same pattern is Lafayette, Louisiana, Detective Randy Comeaux.

"It's a very similar case. He was also a cop and a criminal profiler in the 1990s," Arntfield said. "He was also a serial rapist. And the same thing – a woman would go into the shower, and he would be holding the flashlight in the same place as DeAngelo would.

"And he also spoke in a very specific way. The detectives were like, 'Do you think this is a cop?' And it turns out Comeaux is following the investigation."

Known as the "South Side Rapist", Comeaux was a former sheriff's deputy who ended up with the Lafayette Police Department. He would later confess to raping 14 women.

And as he raped and molested the terrified women, Comeaux would threaten them with his service gun. Little to no forensic evidence was ever left behind at the scene during the two-decade span of the twisted cop's crimes.

But the Comeaux probe was also the first known use of geographic profiling in a criminal investigation to zero in on the rapist's hunting grounds.

In the end it was an anonymous tip and DNA from a discarded cigarette butt that led sex crimes detectives to Comeaux. He was convicted and is now serving a life sentence.

Geography is also a factor, as addressed in earlier chapters, in the case of the Golden State Killer. California, of course, has never lacked serial murderers. Arntfield has several theories on why the Golden West has so many monsters.

"I mean, there are some theories that there was a correlation between climate and serial crime, where the warmer temperatures make mobility easier," he said. "That would also mean a greater likelihood of target availability."

The warmer western climate makes life easier for transients, many of whom are running from trouble in the east.

"You can understand it if you've been to Napa and San Francisco. You can see that you can live better on the street in San Francisco than you can in Canada with a house," Arntfield said.

The place and the times play a crucial role.

"A lot of things were going on at the time in California. Cults, drugs, the weather and just a massive movement to settle out there. Part of it's also just a product of the large population," Arntfield noted.

For decades following the Second World War, America was on the move, and the final destination was more often than not California. In recent years, that's changed, particularly because of the polarization of the American electorate and other factors, including taxation.

"There's been less interstate movement in the last few years because people are so politically divided. They're saying, 'No, I'm not taking on a transfer to Birmingham, Alabama.' They're saying, 'I'm staying in Little Rock,'" Arntfield said.

"The one exception is people moving out of California. U-Haul has logged more one-way trips out-of-state from California over the last five years than anywhere else. What a great metric – you rent a truck in San Diego and drop it off in Dallas."

The nation's most populous state has been swamped over the past decade by an epidemic of crime, homelessness and high taxes that have made California less appealing.

"They keep track of all that. They're not coming back. And California politicians are saying, 'Oh, nobody's coming in,' and everyone's renting them in California, scattering all over the country. And that's because it's a state of people who are out of control."

Joseph DeAngelo left only crumbs and heartache in his murderous wake. There is not much of a footprint to try and get to the depths of his dark soul.

But other serial killers have been captured, tried and studied. The Golden State Killer ticks a slew of psychological boxes.

"This is why all these serial killers have certain common characteristics from childhood. The isolation of constantly moving, of not having the family resources to have friends over, and the humiliation of an overbearing and neglectful or abusive parent," Arntfield said.

"They spend a lot of time alone, retreating into their fantasy world as they begin to get older."

During the 2020−22 COVID pandemic, mental health issues exploded. Triggering many of the breakdowns was often loneliness and limited contact with the outside world.

"That whole period really revealed people's underlying true nature," Arntfield said.

"People were driving in their cars with a mask on by themselves, and you know it doesn't work anyway. But that becomes part of the compulsion that they have to go through this ritual before they leave the house; they have to be safe."

Rituals like those performed by lonely men who once had been abused little boys and, like the Golden State Killer, grew up to be something else.

8

Escalation

The winds of change were rapidly approaching the California of the 1970s. Things were evolving for Joseph James DeAngelo as well.

The divisive Vietnam War was in the rearview mirror, and the hippies and other transients who flooded into California in their hundreds of thousands in the 1960s were getting jobs and settling down. Flower Power was dead and about to be overtaken by the Greed is Good ethos, even in the flaky Golden State.

The stage was set for the emergence of Ronald Reagan and Margaret Thatcher.

Late in 1979, the world was riveted, starting on 4 November, when 500 Iranian radicals invaded the US Embassy in Tehran. They would take 90 hostages, including 53 Americans. Earlier in the year, the Shah of Iran had been deposed. In his place was the pious, sinister theocrat Ayatollah Khomeini. The students were demanding that the US return the Shah to Iran to stand trial.

Disco ruled the airwaves and the nightlife, with people grooving to Donna Summer, Gloria Gaynor, Chic, the Village People and The Knack.

At home, people were watching *Three's Company*, *Alice*, *MASH* and *Dallas* on TV. At the cinema, the surreal Vietnam War blockbuster *Apocalypse Now* led the box office, along with *Alien* and *Escape from Alcatraz*.

The year 1979 was also the year that changed Mary Berwert's life forever. The 13-year-old earned a desired position on the Walnut Creek cheerleading squad. Two months later, her life would be thrown into turmoil.

Walnut Creek in Contra Costa County is about 70 miles (113 km) southwest of Sacramento. It is considered part of the San Francisco Bay Area.

Formerly a small farming community, in the post-war years, its population exploded as suburban tracts sprang up among the former orchards. In 1950, around 2,500 people called the area home. Thirty years later, there were nearly 70,000 residents.

Two members of the famed heavy metal band Metallica grew up in the leafy, temperate area, as did Baseball Hall of Fame pitcher Randy "The Big Unit" Johnson.

But into this suburban idyll, evil came calling on 25 June 1979, and Mary Berwert became one of the youngest victims of Joseph James DeAngelo.

Around 4 a.m., a man slipped into the teen's bedroom. No one heard a peep. The invader put a sharp knife against her throat.

"He tied my hands and my legs and gagged me with my training bra. And he raped me. And he said he was going to look for money in the rest of my house and, if I said a word, he was going to kill my family," Berwert recalled decades later. "And I just laid there thinking, 'What am I going to do?'"

After around 45 minutes of horror, the girl was able to break her feet loose and sprinted down the hall to raise the alarm with her father. Her 16-year-old sister across the hall heard nothing.

She would later recall the look on her dad's face as "devastating" as he dialled the cops. In the kitchen, she grabbed a sharp knife out of a drawer to defend herself to the death if the evil phantom was still in the home.

Officers were on the scene in minutes, and their bloodhounds scoured the family's backyard for clues. The next morning, the girl's father tore down a cherished playhouse where Berwert and her sister had frolicked when they were young children.

"That's where he was watching me, stalking me. Lying on top of the playhouse, he could see right into my bedroom window," Berwert said.

Her tight-knit neighbourhood was terror-stricken with fears that the rapist could return and ravage another child.

As crime began spiking in America's big cities in the post-war era, many families retreated to the quiet of the suburbs. A place where they would be safe and, more importantly, their children would not be walking targets.

The epidemic of serial rape – soon followed by serial murder – was partly the result of the seeming safety of the suburbs. People developed a false sense of security. Violent crime and unrest were for the crumbling inner cities.

But as in the nation's great metropolises, neighbours didn't know each other. And they didn't want to get involved.

At the time, it became known as the Kitty Genovese effect after a Queens, NY barmaid who was brutally murdered in 1964 while her neighbours seemingly did nothing. Only in the past decade has that myth – largely the creation of *The New York Times* – been shattered. Genovese's neighbours DID rush to her rescue, and many did, in fact, call the police. But for decades, myth became reality.

And suburbia became the prime hunting grounds for the new generation of serial rapists like the East Area Rapist.

People kept to themselves, there were few streetlights, 911 was in the future, and there was very little home security. And there was no DNA technology, rendering many forensic clues null and void.

In the Sacramento area, there were at least four serial rapists operating in the 1970s. One of these sex fiends raped 42 women but received only the barest of media mentions. Rape investigations were often cursory at best. And there was still a pervasive attitude in police precincts and the courts that maybe the victim deserved it.

And when there was a conviction, the rapist might face no more than a year in prison. Even if detectives were diligent, the window to bring the matter to court was brief due to the statute of limitations. As a result, evidence was often trashed.

The attitude was exemplified by a criminal profiler's description of the East Area Rapist as "gentlemanly".

Media also fell asleep at the wheel – until reporters and editors could no longer turn away.

As details of the East Area Rapist began emerging, initially at a community meeting, real fear escalated along with sales of guns, locks and dogs.

But police were tight-lipped, keeping details of the attacks and the predator's modus operandi a closely guarded secret. Attempts were made to stifle media coverage.

In the suburban Sacramento neighbourhoods where the East Area Rapist prowled, officers were stunned during canvassing to hear residents claim they heard scratching at their back door. They had even seen the phantom. But why stir up trouble? So, they didn't call the cops.

According to the *Los Angeles Times*, one teen girl spotted a strange man in the backyard of a neighbour's home. She closed her drapes and said nothing. The same night, her neighbour was raped.

And cops themselves seemed to imply that residents were on their own. A neighbourhood watch was organized, and in the East Area Rapist's stomping grounds, a vigilante posse armed with guns wandered the streets.

Finally, law enforcement formed a 100-officer "rape squad" to patrol the quiet suburban streets. They were given orders that they were to shoot to kill if they encountered the monster. Likewise, the message to residents was don't hesitate to park a bullet in this guy.

One itchy-fingered resident sent a burglar to the morgue. He was cleared because of the public panic.

But the East Area Rapist was different from the others. He lingered. He tormented his victims. He inflicted grievous psychological torture. And he raped his victims multiple times.

The quarry wasn't simply a freak. He was cunning, he was prepared, he was studious.

The East Area Rapist had studied his victims well. He knew their schedules and those of their neighbours, husbands and children.

His pre-rape rites included preparing the crime scene. He would break in and unlock doors and windows. And as a precaution, if there was a gun in the house, the rapist would remove the bullets. In addition, he would stash cords around the home to bind his victims when he struck in the wee hours of the morning.

Typically, his preferred location to make his presence known was the bedroom where his prey slept. At first, his targets were lone women and girls before moving on to moms with children sleeping in the home. Finally, and deadliest, he began attacking women whose husbands or boyfriends were present.

It wasn't enough for DeAngelo to rape, torture and torment his female victims. He also relished emasculating his victims' male partners.

His opening gambit after terrifying his victims was to assuage their fears. He only wanted money or maybe food. That's it. And then he would leave, he assured them.

DeAngelo went to almost absurd lengths to lay a false trail for cops, making it appear like he was a drifter or a kid from the neighbourhood. Once he planted evidence from another home.

But once the East Area Rapist was in control of the situation, he would bind his victims, turn them face down, and often gag them with bras. He would then scour the house looking for whatever turned his crank.

He would tell them, "Make the bed twinge," or, "I'll kill you." To another he spat out, "I'll butcher you all to pieces."

"Make one move," he snarled at one victim, "and you'll be silent forever."

And then he would return with that peculiar sex-driven look in his eyes. Victims said the rapist seemed sexually insatiable, sometimes raping them nine times during an attack. The fiend would then take a break, maybe prowl the house some more or grab a bite or a beer in the kitchen.

He would then rape the victim once more. He would skip taking valuables, items worth real money. Instead, he took cash, coins and trophies. Knick-knacks, wedding bands, rings, earrings, and other items to celebrate his twisted triumph.

Even as an epidemic of rapes plagued Sacramento, the relationship between women's groups and cops was fraught with distrust. One detective shockingly told the city's two newspapers, *The Sacramento Bee* and *The Sacramento Union*, that the counsellors from the rape centre were anti-male lesbians.

The situation between the cops and women's groups became so strained that the sheriff blocked funding to the crisis centre. He refused to work with the women working there, even when he had been ordered to do so.

On the other side of the coin, an executive at the centre slammed the sheriff as a "pig" and accused him of covering up details about the rapist and leaving local women with targets painted on their backs.

Odds were steep that detectives could not catch the East Area Rapist unless they nabbed him in the middle of an attack. California statistics painted a bleak picture of the possibility of a conviction.

Just one in 16 rapes resulted in a conviction. Detection was entirely a different matter, particularly for a cunning predator like Joseph DeAngelo. Things were so bad that cops in San Jose barely bothered to investigate rape unless the victim was acquainted with her attacker.

When DeAngelo began hunting in San Jose, cops gave only a half-hearted attempt at investigation. Two local EAR attacks were discovered almost by accident.

"I don't think rape was considered the horrendous crime that it is considered today," retired EAR task force leader Ray Root told the *Los Angeles Times*, adding he cringes when he looks back. Rape, he said, was considered "just another physical assault".

Shockingly, out of a staggering 9,522 reported rapes in 1976 in California, just 573 resulted in convictions. And even a guilty verdict meant only a year, and maybe less, in the local jail. Some were released directly to probation.

Finally, in 1978, forcible rape became an offence that carried heavier time. Three years in prison may not seem like a lot, but it was a marked improvement. Still, the biggest roadblock was the meagre statute of limitations on rape. Just three years in some cases.

And as the East Area Rapist ramped up his deviant crusade, the statute of limitations passed on many of his earlier crimes.

The fear, tears and horror were about to reach new depths. Joseph DeAngelo was going to up the stakes and take his show on the road. In his sick mind, rape was no longer enough.

By late 1979, he had murdered three people. No one made any connections at that point.

Goleta, California, in Santa Barbara County, north of Los Angeles, is 387 miles (623 km) south of Sacramento, close to a six-hour drive. Its most famous native is pop singer Katy Perry.

The quiet beach town has around 55,000 people and is far from the hustle and bustle of LA. It is mostly white, mostly well-off and mostly safe. Murder is a rare thing indeed.

Why Joseph DeAngelo strayed so far from his normal hunting grounds remains a puzzle.

But on Monday, 1 October 1979, he landed on Queen Ann Lane in Goleta with malice in his heart and his bloodlust raging. There had already been a series of mostly minor break-ins in the area that autumn, along with one assault. On that first night in October, the predator chose a home along a tree-lined creek on Goleta's outskirts.

A hooded intruder entered the residence in a scene that had been repeated dozens of times in and around the California capital. The prowler employed virtually the same methodology as the East Area Rapist.

The criminal startled a sleeping couple and forced the woman to bind her boyfriend. He then dragged her to the living room. In the kitchen, the crazed attacker ranted almost as if it were his mantra: "I'll kill 'em, I'll kill 'em, I'll kill 'em."

The victim said that the culprit uttered the terrifying phrase no less than 12 times. Miraculously, the couple got loose and managed to escape. A neighbour heard them screaming and responded. The intruder fled into the night and likely onto US Highway 101, where he headed north, back to Citrus Heights.

Of course, the shaken couple had no way of knowing who had invaded their home. A mask in the dark. That was it.

Already the same monster had raped dozens of women in the Sacramento area. And less than two years earlier, he claimed his second and third victims when he murdered Katie and Brian Maggiore in February 1978 as they walked their dog.

But suddenly, in Sacramento and the Bay Area, the East Area Rapist went quiet. To investigators, it wasn't clear whether the EAR was dead or in prison. As a result, cops began winding down the investigation in Sacramento. In Contra Costa, detectives were urged to back off when the rapes that had plagued the county suddenly stopped.

Only the most forward-thinking investigator could know that Joseph DeAngelo was poised to make the quantum leap from rapist to serial killer. The unidentified Goleta couple had escaped with their lives. That game was now over.

There had been scouting expeditions to Goleta, and cops later found strands of nylon rope in the Queen Ann Lane area, but those sojourns were likely for reconnaissance purposes.

His foray on Sunday, 30 December 1979, however, was not about scouting targets. It was not a drill. There would be murder on the menu.

On that night, DeAngelo broke into at least seven residences and performed his usual rituals of ransacking bedrooms, stealing jewellery and attacking dogs. There was something different in store for the eighth house.

It was a temperate morning in Goleta that day. Warm enough for tennis but not sweltering.

William and Joan Oakley had a mixed doubles date with osteopathic surgeon Dr Robert Offerman and his new girlfriend, psychiatrist Dr Debra Alexandria Manning. But something seemed off at Offerman's condominium, located at 767 Avenida Pequena.

William Oakley noticed that one of the sliding glass doors at the condo was open. Stepping inside, the couple called out to Offerman, but there was no response. Oakley explored further, moving deeper into the house when he was met by a horrific sight.

Crossing the living room and looking down the hall, he saw a female body on the bed.

"There's a girl lying on the bed naked," Oakley reportedly told his wife, who believed they were interrupting Offerman and his girlfriend having sex and wanted to go.

William Oakley was ready to cut out, too. But something nagged at him. His friend would have answered after he called out, in bed having sex or not. He then turned around and went to the bedroom to verify whether the sick suspicions gnawing at his guts were true.

Sheriff's deputies arrived a short time later. "There are two people dead inside," Joan Oakley said, sobbing.

On the right side of the waterbed was Alexandria Manning. Her wrists were bound behind her back with white nylon twine. Offerman was on his knees, as if praying, at the foot of the bed.

In his hand, he was clutching twine.

Cops theorized that because of pry marks on the windows, the killer had used a screwdriver to make his entrance. And if the MO stood, he struck in the wee hours of the morning while the occupants slept.

No doubt he pointed a gun at the sleepy lovebirds. He was there to rob them, he likely told the pair. But being cautious, he no doubt ordered Manning to bind Offerman with the twine.

Detectives believe that Manning did not tie her boyfriend's wrists very tightly, perhaps loosely enough so that he could get loose and escape. Offerman then likely broke free and tried to put up a fight.

Around 3 a.m., neighbours reported hearing gunshots from Offerman's condo. Then a pause. Then another gunshot. The popular doctor was shot three times in the back and chest. Manning was killed with a single bullet to the back of her head.

Investigators discovered two of Manning's rings that appeared to have been slipped between the mattress and the bed frame to conceal them. On the nightstand on Offerman's side of the bed, there was the never-to-be-finished book, *Your Perfect Right: A Guide to Assertive Behavior* by Robert E. Alberti.

The crime scene was also eerily festive. There was the wreath festooned with red flowers, a Christmas tree parked in the hall. More chilling were the remains of the holiday turkey, wrapped in Saran Wrap (cling film) left on the patio.

It looked like the killer had worked up an appetite in the wake of his sinister activities.

An intensive search of the area turned up evidence of a prowler who had roamed the neighbourhood, looking for opportunity and then striking. There was a trampled flower bed at the condo next to Offerman's.

Inside the unit, there was evidence of a squatter living there. Most obviously in the bathroom, where strands of the white twine were also left behind.

Prints from the killer's Adidas tennis shoes were all around the exterior of the death house, as if Offerman's condo had been circled multiple times.

Cops later received reports that there had been a number of ransackings and break-ins in the area that Saturday night and early into Sunday morning. Nearby, another couple had spotted a burglar racing through their living room to the back door.

That was around 10:15 p.m.

They heard him jump over the back fence, and then he was gone. Their description was vague: Caucasian, wearing a dark jacket and a fisherman's hat. He'd also brutally punched their poodle in the eye.

Crime was not unheard of, but rare in Goleta, eight miles (13 km) west of downtown Santa Barbara. Murder was out of the question.

As the investigation intensified, more pieces of the mysterious nylon twine were discovered in yards and trails in the area. Two months prior, another couple on Queen Ann Lane had narrowly missed meeting the same fate as Offerman and Manning.

"In mid-'78, he moved down to the East Bay into my jurisdiction, and those were the files that I was looking at," retired investigator Paul Holes said.

"And I was hooked 'cause as I read the victim's statements about what this offender was doing to them, what he was saying to them, the fact that he was going into the middle of the night and attacking couples, a man and a woman, I recognized that the psychology of this offender was very different than the typical serial rapist."

He added: "This was a much bolder and more brazen offender than what I had even read in the *Sexual Homicide* book."

9

A Double Murder in Ventura

The year 1979 would go down as a watershed in the life of Joseph DeAngelo.

In many ways, it was his *annus horribilis*.

In his guise as the East Area Rapist, he had continued terrorizing the Sacramento area but suddenly stopped his reign of terror that had turned the city into a landscape of fear.

On the second-to-last day of the year, he switched his ample energies to murder nearly six hours south in Goleta in Santa Barbara County. On 30 December 1979, as detailed earlier, he murdered Dr Robert Offerman and Dr Debra Alexandria Manning in the early morning hours.

They would be marked as the fourth and fifth victims of the Golden State Killer. There would be many more deaths to come.

In July that year, DeAngelo was pinched stealing at a hardware store and inevitably was fired from the job that meant everything to him. The power of a badge and a gun was like rocket fuel for the Vietnam vet. And then it was gone.

Ironically, DeAngelo wasn't much of a cop.

"No significant arrests. No significant citations," retired Auburn Police Chief Nick Willick told the *Los Angeles Times*, adding he was "unremarkable".

He did the duties of a typical small-town cop: parade duty, parking, delinquent kids, traffic and other minor but necessary duties. DeAngelo often worked the overnight shift.

Fellow cops called DeAngelo "Junk Food Joey" for his addiction to chips and soda. The best way to describe the new cop would be maladroit. He was awkward and did make attempts to be a team player, but it didn't really work.

"He wasn't an outstanding police officer. He really wasn't," Willick said.

One of the key components of small-town police work is connecting with people and becoming part of the community. Being a hard ass does not work.

One resident complained about the new cop's "attitude". When Willick watched his officer write a minor citation, he was shocked as he watched the burly DeAngelo get in the guy's face even as he stepped backwards.

Willick later had a few words with DeAngelo, telling him to ease up. His disposition was making the taxpayers nervous. The police chief noted that his in-your-face style also wasn't safe. That closeness offered up an opportunity for the desperate and unhinged person to grab his revolver and put DeAngelo in a pine box.

That wouldn't be DeAngelo's last dressing down. Once, the officer, now in his early thirties, slipped away while he was supposed to be on patrol. He claimed he had taken a coffee break at home.

Willick said, "He did not take criticism well. He wouldn't get angry. He would pout like a little kid, and he'd sulk."

After he was busted for shoplifting in July, it was a no-brainer for Willick to fire the mediocre cop. On the spot. His bounty? A hammer and a can of dog repellent. But the two clerks had to tie him to a chair in a back room of the store until police arrived.

If Willick thought that was going to be the end of DeAngelo, he had another think coming. The disgraced cop made a work-related injury claim against the City of Auburn. DeAngelo claimed Willick had harassed him to the point of a nervous breakdown.

Not long after, there was the incident where the chief found his toddler daughter lying on the floor beside his bed. She saw a man at her bedroom window. He was shining a flashlight.

Willick investigated. There were footprints under the window, but he chalked it up to construction workers still toiling on his house. The man in the window? A bad nightmare.

The top cop left it at that. But an insurance man for the city, who was investigating Joseph DeAngelo's claim, told Willick that the fired cop admitted to him that he went to his ex-boss's house with a gun.

He wanted to kill the chief but could not find a suitable entryway into the house. Willick blew it off as part of a cash grab from his former employer and left DeAngelo in the rearview mirror.

His young daughter, though, lived with nightmares for years of the man peering into her window.

The Sacramento area was getting increasingly too hot for the East Area Rapist. Continuing his prowling there was untenable. Necessity meant the sex fiend needed to move further afield, west towards the Bay Area and south into populous Southern California.

Survivors told cops that the EAR appeared to be becoming increasingly unglued. He wept and cursed his "Mommy", and one even recalled that he whispered, "Bonnie" – the name of his former fiancée. And he would gasp for air during attacks, more ritual than physical necessity.

But it was looking as though the EAR's reign of terror was beginning to ebb. Just as quickly as they had begun, the rapes suddenly stopped. Maybe he had aged out of his evil activities or had moved on.

Either way, police bureaucrats were anxious to shut down the pricey investigations that devoured money and manpower with abandon.

The Sacramento EAR task force was largely disbanded. In Contra Costa, investigators were ordered to "stand down" when the sex attacks stopped there.

And then Contra Costa Lieutenant Larry Crompton became aware of the double murder and close encounter further south, in Goleta, on 30 December 1979. He tipped off his counterpart in Sacramento. Two Sacramento County detectives made the pilgrimage to Santa Barbara County to determine how much the killer further south had in common with their man.

According to media reports, after scouring the police reports on the Goleta double murder and attempted assault, the detective determined the crimes were also the work of the East Area Rapist. His boss, Lieutenant Ray Root, disagreed with the detective's assessment.

Root later told the *Los Angeles Times* that whereas the Sacramento rapist was fastidious, the Goleta killer seemed to be a sloppy amateur. The East Area Rapist never lost control of his victims. If this were the same guy, surely his skills would have improved.

Investigators in Santa Barbara were anxious to combine efforts to nab the killer rapist. They made overtures to Sacramento for a joint probe and a merging of resources. But Root said he didn't think linking the cases was a particularly good idea. For starters, heightened media coverage could send the rapist into the woodwork.

Cops are naturally averse to using the words serial rapist or serial killer. It could trigger hysteria among an already panicked public. No, it was decided to keep a lid on things.

Detectives were ordered to keep quiet about the most recent attack in the state capital. The brass did not want an overreaction by the media that would surely make things worse. Santa Barbara authorities knew this better than their colleagues in Sacramento.

As former movie star and California Governor Ronald Reagan began making plans to run for president, the hub of his ambition was at his ranch outside Goleta.

Local law enforcement had only recently put another serial killer in the rearview mirror. The maniac dumped one of his victim's bodies outside the gates of Reagan's ranch.

During late 1976 and early 1977, the University of California in Santa Barbara was terrorized by a macabre killer. The slayings were labelled the "Look-Alike Murders" because the victims bore an uncanny resemblance to each other.

Co-ed Jacqueline Rook, 21, was abducted from a bus stop in Goleta on 6 December 1976. Goleta waitress Mary Sarris disappeared the same day; the details of her abduction are murkier.

Both were still missing on 18 January 1977 when Patricia Laney, 21, vanished from another local bus stop. Laney's corpse was discovered the next day in nearby Refugio Canyon, the location of Reagan's ranch. Detectives were alive to the twisted pattern when they discovered Rook dead in the same area on 20 January.

The women looked much alike, and they all died the same way: with a single bullet to the head from a small-calibre handgun.

Thor Nis Christiansen, 22, had the shaggy look of a California surfer, although he had immigrated from Denmark as a child. Christiansen first came to the cops' attention in February 1977 as part of a large round-up of people questioned in the shocking homicides.

Detectives ruled him out as a suspect, just a teen punk with booze on his breath, even though they confiscated a .22-calibre handgun from his car.

On 22 May 1977, the remains of Mary Sarris were discovered in Drum Canyon, north of Santa Barbara. Investigators did not give Christiansen another thought, but the killer himself was not quite ready to leave the stage.

On 26 May 1979, the body of 22-year-old Laura Benjamin was discovered in a drainage culvert near Big Tujunga Dam in the Angeles National Forest. She had likely been killed sometime in April with two gunshots to the head.

On 18 April 1979, a 24-year-old woman named Lydia Preston was hitchhiking in the Hollywood area when Christiansen offered her a lift. Several blocks after letting her into his car, he pulled the gun and fired a bullet into her left ear.

Soaked in blood, Preston jumped from the car, saving herself and escaping. But three months later, Preston spotted her attacker in a Hollywood watering hole. She quickly called LA County Sheriff's deputies, who arrested Christiansen for felonious assault.

Cops in Santa Barbara saw the missive on the police wire and noted similarities between their murders and the Hollywood attack. They also discovered he had been pinched for drunk driving on 7 July, and that at that time, officers had seized another .22-calibre handgun.

He was charged in late July with three counts of first-degree murder in Santa Barbara. Charges of first-degree murder and attempted murder followed in Los Angeles.

A psychiatric evaluation of Christiansen revealed he suffered from an "intermittent explosive disorder", a paranoid personality, chronic drug use and necrophilia. Christiansen told detectives he killed his victims, took them to a secluded place, stripped them naked, and sexually explored their bodies.

He was sentenced to 25 years to life for the murder of Laura Benjamin and nine years for the attempted murder of Lydia Preston.

Less than a month later, he went on trial for the trio of Santa Barbara murders. He pleaded guilty after six of seven psychiatrists in Los Angeles found that he was sane. He was sentenced to life in prison.

He didn't last long in prison. Thor Christiansen was stabbed to death at Folsom State Prison on 30 March 1981 in the exercise yard. His killer has never been identified.

In the golden age of serial killers, it wasn't surprising that law enforcement was exercising caution in linking violent crimes hundreds of miles away.

Sacramento Sheriff's Homicide Lieutenant Ray Root told the Santa Barbara Sheriff: "If you want to connect those rapes and homicides, then stand by. Because that's what you'll get."

Many investigators in the three areas where the Golden State Killer hunted had already done the math and concluded the rapes and murders were indeed connected. Still, Root was not convinced and didn't think a multi-jurisdictional task force was the way forward.

Eventually, the top cops in Sacramento and Santa Barbara came to the same conclusion.

Police even floated a story to the Sacramento newspapers that the East Area Rapist and the Goleta Creek Killer were not the same person. They may have jumped the gun.

Ventura County is sandwiched between Santa Barbara County to the north and Los Angeles County to the south. Easy access to myriad freeways makes it ideal for a serial killer to get in and out of the areas quickly.

The next victims of the Original Night Stalker (later the Golden State Killer) would be Lyman and Charlene Smith. Around two-and-a-half months after the shocking murders of Dr Robert Offerman and Dr Debra Alexandria Manning, at Offerman's Goleta condo, the killer struck again.

On Thursday, 13 March 1980, the Smiths were discovered in their stylish Ventura home about 40 minutes south of Goleta and more than six hours south of Sacramento. Cops guessed the couple had been dead for two days.

One neighbour thought it was bizarre that there appeared to be a milk carton on the counter every time she looked over at the Smiths' kitchen window. Lyman Smith's 12-year-old son from his first marriage found the bodies when he arrived to mow the lawn.

According to cops, the couple had been bludgeoned and then bound with a comforter covering them. Investigators again discovered a blood-covered fire log, much like the kind of crude weapon used to kill the dogs not that long ago in Rancho Cordova.

Detectives discovered evidence at the crime scene indicating that Charlene Smith had been raped. For years, police blew it off, telling the couple's daughter and reporters that Charlene had not been raped. Again, there was a fear that a major media announcement would panic the public and drive the killer underground.

Ironically, decades later it was a vaginal swab taken from Charlene's body that provided the DNA that would link the murders to several rapes.

Ventura County detectives were not looking for a statewide super predator, though. Their efforts zeroed in on perceived local villains. One of the persons of interest on their radar was a business partner of Lyman Smith.

Smith was on the cusp of being promoted to a Ventura County Superior Court judge, and he expected an announcement any day. It would be a culmination of Smith's ambition and intensity. One individual had lost a fortune in a business deal with Lyman that went sideways.

Cops were certain that the killer knew Lyman Smith, the likely target. But if so, why would they go to the trouble of murdering his wife, Charlene? How the couple died was equally telling. They had been bludgeoned to death, and if the ex-business partner was the killer, wouldn't he have used a gun?

In addition, business dispute murders rarely, if ever, end with a spouse being raped. Lyman was also heavily involved with the county's Democratic Party machine and numerous business deals, some of them controversial.

Investigators were also looking closely at the couple's private life. Charlene, 33, was a decade younger than Lyman, and although the couple were reportedly happy, both had sexual affairs outside the marriage. Her lover was also briefly a suspect.

Cops quickly returned to their favourite suspect: Lyman's former business partner, Joseph Alsip Jr. Alsip's finances had taken a beating in a failed business deal with Lyman. Two years after the murders, he was arrested, convincing many that the case was done and dusted.

It was not. Still, it was easy to see why the police focused on Lyman's business dealings as the trigger for his demise.

"Lyman was a little bit intense," a friend told a Ventura County newspaper. "Very intelligent, very able and knowledgeable, but a little intense, like a lot of people who want to be a millionaire at a young age."

The friend added, "He had a desire to make money quickly, and was a little aggressive, doing too much and getting in over his head."

The above attitudes were the things police were looking at. Who were Lyman Smith's enemies? Former business partners, for starters.

"Lyman was smart, but he should have taken it easier … he could have done great things if he had taken it a little easier."

Still, it never entered the minds of his friends and acquaintances that Lyman and Charlene were murdered by a serial killer.

His friend added: "I kept thinking, 'who finally got mad enough at him to kill Lyman and his wife like that?' But never did I think of a serial killer. Now, I guess it makes some sick sense."

At one point, police went so far as to file charges against Lyman Smith's aggrieved business partner. He was eventually cleared of any wrongdoing.

Detectives also put the spotlight on the couple's teen daughter, Jennifer Carole. She even took a polygraph. At the time, it didn't make any sense to her. Jennifer Carole noted that she couldn't rape anyone.

It was the DNA found in her stepmother that would eventually close the case.

"A sexual assault kit from Charlene Smith was obtained from the coroner's office, and we were able to get the Golden State Killer's DNA out of that sexual assault kit," retired Contra Costa District Attorney investigator Paul Holes said.

"That was the DNA sample that we used in order to generate a profile that ultimately led to Joseph DeAngelo."

Decades later, Jennifer Carole remains haunted by the horrific crime.

"My mom came home with my youngest brother, Gary, who had found my dad and Charlene in their home. He had gone up to mow the lawn," she recalled to KCRA.

"When they came home, Gary ran right into his bedroom. He just ran straight, and I could tell he was crying. My mom said, 'Your dad is dead.' I just didn't believe it at first, and then she said, 'And Charlene is, too.'"

She recalled that her brother entered the home trying to get access to the garage and found it odd that the alarm clock was buzzing. Digital clocks of the era buzzed until you turned them off.

"At first, he was worried, like, oh privacy, like they could be just waking up, but it didn't make sense because he was there around noon," Carole said.

"So he went ahead and went back there, and that's when he saw there were two people under a comforter, and the clock, which was over on my dad's side of the bed on his nightstand, was going off. So Gary went over to just shut the clock off and to see what was going on."

She added, "He essentially went in and looked at the comforter and could tell that it was my dad right away and knew that something bad had happened."

To this day, her younger brother has not talked about the murders and his gruesome discovery at the dawn of the 1980s.

"It's almost a cliche how much the MO is the same when you look at the murders. I can see how they were able to put this suspicion together and then link it through DNA. It's because the MO was very similar," she said.

"Somebody broke into the house. My dad was bound, Charlene was bound as well. She was absolutely brutally raped, repeatedly, is how as I understand it, and then she was – both of them were bludgeoned. It was a murder scene that was found at least a day later."

She likened the trauma to those who witnessed the shocking terrorist attacks on 9/11 – the horror is there, but also not knowing what was going on.

"So if you think about when those planes hit the Twin Towers, most of us were angry, afraid, crying and screaming, and at the same time, not understanding at all what was happening, like it just didn't make any sense," she explained. "That is exactly how it feels.

"It doesn't make sense, and you having feelings, but you're not even sure what to attach them to, other than the sadness that you have because somebody is dead. But even then, it's so fresh you don't – it doesn't really go."

For the public in Ventura, with its proximity to Los Angeles, there wasn't the same sense of panic and paranoia as there had been in Sacramento. But to those aware of the evil unfolding in their midst, it was sheer, stark terror.

"I became scared, and I think I was scared because I wasn't sure if the person that had killed my dad and Charlene wanted to get even with him, maybe and get his whole family," Lyman Smith's daughter said.

"So I was scared in that way, but in no way did it affect the community in terms of there's a murderer on the loose. It seemed so personal and so directed at them, and to find out later that it was random, of course, it's just one of the reasons it's mind-blowing."

But like the other murders, the double slaying of Lyman and Charlene Smith went cold fast, the gruesome details packed away in boxes in the basements of police stations.

A cunning predator faded once more into the abyss, and police seemed helpless when bringing to heel the ravenous dog preying on quiet, upper-class communities.

As the decades passed, Jennifer Carole admitted she didn't think cops would ever catch her father's killer. Nor did she know that the man responsible was a serial killer and serial rapist.

"I, like so many, had followed true crime since my dad's murder, and I have been interested in it and understood that to be killed by a serial killer, it's right up there almost with lightning strikes," Carole said.

"You know it's very, very unusual. It's incredibly unusual, so that essentially blew my mind," adding that she was stunned by the DNA science that brought the killer to justice.

"The minute I knew we had his DNA connection, he was caught in my mind. We just may not have had the person but we knew we'd have him when we got him.

"The DNA that they used, that Paul Holes used to match and that they used to make the arrest, was from, as I understand it, was from my stepmother's body. That's really significant for me, and it's powerful for me to know that at least there was some way she was able to help solve the crime."

But the back-slapping would be far into the future.

For decades, there would be little to celebrate in the Golden State Killer investigation.

One investigator summed up for *The Atlantic* magazine why this psychotic menace was so difficult to catch: "Poor communication between agencies, investigative tunnel vision and antiquated technology."

10

The Night Stalker

The tumultuous 1970s were spent, exhausted by ten years of excess. But on the final day, the calendar flipped to the spanking new decade of the 1980s. Sex, drugs and rock and roll had burned the Me Decade to a crisp. It was time for something new.

In the wake of Vietnam, the 1973 energy crisis and massive social, political and economic upheaval, America was ready to move on and get a fresh start.

Punk, new wave and classic rock were kicking disco to the kerb. But that August, mellow masters Olivia Newton-John and Christopher Cross ruled the Top 40 charts. On TV, *Dallas*, *The Dukes of Hazzard*, and *60 Minutes* were the most watched shows in the US.

That season would bring the eternal question: Who shot J.R.?

On the big screen, *Smokey and the Bandit II* topped the domestic box office, followed by *Xanadu* and *The Octagon*.

Joseph DeAngelo was ready for a fresh start, too. He had retired both the Visalia Ransacker and the East Area Rapist who had terrorized Sacramento and surrounding areas. It was time for something new, something more daring.

His new guise was more cunning, more brutal, more terrifying. And he was on the move to new hunting grounds in Southern California.

After murdering Dr Robert Offerman and Dr Debra Alexandria Manning at Offerman's condo in Goleta in Santa Barbara County on 30 December 1979, the killer moved south again. The next to die were Charlene and Lyman Smith, who were murdered in their Ventura County home on 13 March 1980.

His next stop would be Dana Point, in suburban Orange County, south of Los Angeles.

Orange County was the sort of landscape the Golden State Killer thrived in. It was suburban, with easy access to numerous freeways, and community planning that appeared designed for a murderer to slip in and out of victims' yards.

Suburbia also gave its denizens a false sense of security. Doors and windows were left unlocked, accompanied by a lackadaisical approach to home security, leaving suburbanites sitting ducks for predators like the Golden State Killer.

Dana Point is nestled along the Pacific Ocean, a wealthy enclave away from the hustle and bustle of Los Angeles. It is considered one of the premier surfing spots on the California coast and attracts thousands to ride the waves every weekend.

Surfing has been the cornerstone of Dana Point for decades. The world's first surf shop opened there in 1954, and it is also home to several surfing magazines that chronicle the sport in infinite detail. Filmmaker Bruce Brown lensed his seminal surfing movie, *The Endless Summer* (1966), at Dana Point.

Crime is rare in Dana Point. Homicide is an even rarer beast still.

However, the community has tasted violence. On 6 May 1993, disgruntled former post office employee Mark Richard Hilbun exploded in a rage after he was fired for stalking a female co-worker.

Hilbun first killed his mother and her dog. He next headed to the postal facility where he once worked and shot two former co-workers. One died while the second postie was wounded. During his three-day rampage, he shot and wounded seven other people before he was arrested. Hilbun was sentenced to seven life sentences without parole.

More recently, in Dana Point, in October 2023, three people went out on a boat with the promise of late-night lobster fishing. Just two came back.

Boaters found Tri "James" Minh Dao floating in the harbour. He had been bludgeoned to death over a drug debt by his friend Hoang "Wayne" Xuan Le and his girlfriend Sheila Ritze. Le was sentenced to life in federal prison for the murder, while Ritze was sentenced to almost 22 years for her role in the crime.

The above two incidents were exceptions to the rule of the quiet, good life on offer in Dana Point.

During the 1970s and 1980s, Dana Point was exploding with new construction. Around 5,000 new units were built in both decades, the largest number of new homes in the city's history.

It is the epitome of the California dream that has been sold to the world since the 1930s. For its 33,000 inhabitants, who are 80 per cent white, privileged and wealthy, and reside in its many gated communities, life is very pleasant indeed.

Not much bad ever happened in Dana Point, but in August 1980, that all changed.

Roger Harrington had purchased a property in a gated community in the fashionable Niguel Shores area. Roger bought the home, which had been built in 1972, years before as an investment and sometimes weekend residence, although he preferred being close to his home further north in Long Beach and to his home security business.

The subdivision had around 950 homes situated just north of the famed Pacific Coast Highway. While it was gated and had a security guard, several places allowed a predator easy access to the multitude of homes.

While the houses were nice, the bottom line was the classic real estate trope of location, location, location. Niguel Shores had a double bonus of the warm California sun paired with a sultry breeze coming off the ocean.

In 1980, the home at 3381 Cockleshell Drive, a corner lot, was valued at $300,000 – about $1.2 million in 2025.

By August 1980, Roger Harrington's son, Keith and his new bride, Patrice, were living in the home.

Friends told the *Los Angeles Times* that the Harringtons met at the University of California Irvine Medical Center the year before. Keith was in his third year of medical school and was specializing in emergency medicine. Patrice was working as a pediatric nurse.

Patrice eventually resigned from the medical centre to work for a private family as a nurse.

The couple moved to San Francisco, where Keith was taking special studies courses. They returned to the Laguna Niguel home in the spring.

Keith and Patrice Harrington were now living in the home. But Roger – a self-made millionaire – still enjoyed doing chores around the home with its spectacular views of the ocean.

Brian Brenner, a friend of the Harringtons at UC Irvine, later said Keith was "one of the most brilliant people I ever met; he was fun-loving, full of life, energetic, raring to go all the time."

On Tuesday, 19 August 1980, Roger spent all day at Keith and Patrice's home installing a sprinkler system. Roger left the house at approximately 6 p.m.

His son was 24 years old and his new daughter-in-law was 28. The newlyweds had only been married for three months, and the match had surprised Roger Harrington.

Patrice was older, and his son may have been on the rebound from another long-term relationship. Yet the couple seemed deliriously happy, and everyone agreed that Patrice was a very sweet, caring young woman.

Around 11 p.m. on 19 August 1980, Patrice's sister called. The call lasted around five minutes, likely expedited because the sister was informed that Keith and Patrice were already tucked in for the night.

Sometime between the end of that phone call and 21 August 1980 at 6:30 p.m., the young couple with their lives and dreams ahead of them on a happy, open road were murdered by Joseph DeAngelo.

According to cops, at around 6:30 p.m. on 21 August 1980, Roger Harrington returned to the home on Cockleshell Drive for a pre-planned dinner with the newlyweds. Oddly, the door was locked, so he used his key to enter. He said, "Hello!" several times, but no one answered. To Roger, this didn't make any sense.

Checking the garage, both Keith's and Patrice's cars were there. Moving back into the kitchen, he noticed a bag of groceries, although none were perishable. He moved down the hall to the spare bedroom that the couple used. The door was closed.

The concerned father pensively opened the door and closed it almost as quickly. Then he re-entered.

Roger Harrington had found Keith and Patrice in their bed. The couple had been murdered.

It was a horror show come to life in all its bloody, crimson grotesquerie. There was no blood on his son's side of the bed. Around Patrice, there was blood everywhere, the comforter and pillow soaked with it.

According to police reports, their bodies were lying face down on the bed and were oddly covered by a comforter. Patrice was wearing a robe while her husband was naked. On the bed, there were pieces of brown cord, and a small knotted piece of brown rope had been discarded on the bedroom floor.

Ligature marks were observed on the wrists of both bodies and the ankles of Patrice's body. A slight mark was on Keith's ankle. Patrice slept with her cherished small baby blanket, and it was discovered between the couple's lifeless bodies. In the kitchen, detectives found Patrice's purse, and it was open, along with some pieces of discarded bread lying on the counter.

During an autopsy, it was noted that there were semen stains on the back of Patrice's right leg and on the comforter that covered their bodies. Forensics investigators also performed vaginal swabs.

And there was a small piece of brass embedded in Patrice's skull. However, the murder weapon, believed to be the head of a sprinkler, was in the wind.

Years later, when science caught up to the investigation, researchers discovered a DNA mixture consistent with one major foreign contributor and one minor contributor, her husband, Keith Harrington. The DNA had been generated from the sperm fraction of the vaginal swab.

Cops believed that the killer – Joseph DeAngelo – broke into the Harrington's home with murder and lust in his heart. His goal was to rape Patrice, steal from the couple and then murder them.

First, he bound them then raped Patrice before bludgeoning them to death with multiple blows to the head with a brass sprinkler head he had discovered in the yard from the new sprinkler system. An autopsy found that the couple both died from brain contusions due to massive skull fractures and blunt-force trauma to the head.

Prosecutors later said, "DeAngelo's decision to kill Patrice and Keith Harrington was willful, deliberate, and premeditated, as evidenced by the nature and extent of the fatal injuries inflicted and the fact that the defendant at the time had already committed numerous other killings in a similar fashion. DeAngelo's intent to steal and rape also was demonstrated by evidence found at the scene and the fact that he had already committed a very large number of rapes and thefts in a similar manner."

It would take 40 years to match the DNA to DeAngelo.

One woman told reporters in 2018 that her own house had been ransacked a week before the double murder. The burglar accidentally dropped rare coins that had been stolen from another neighbour. She added that her dog scared off a man trying to break in several nights before the Harrington murders.

Cops have long noted that DeAngelo was big on researching potential victims, frequently casing targets weeks in advance to determine entry points and whether or not his female victims would be alone. He was committed to the craft of murder.

For neighbour Carole Daly, she has never forgotten that terrible day. She lived a block away with her two sons. On the day Roger Harrington discovered his son and daughter-in-law's bodies, her 15-year-old, who had just returned from surfing, told the dark tale.

He told his mother, "Mr Harrington is sitting on the kerb crying, and the police are all around."

Daly said she hit the panic button, locking doors and covering up her home's windows with blankets. She was confused. And she was very afraid.

In the wake of the murders, rumours spread like wildfire. It was drug-related. It was a Mafia takedown. Of course, neither of those rumours nor the scores of others that blossomed like algae in a polluted lake were remotely true.

"There was a lot of suspicion about who did it," said former neighbour John Lee. "They were nice people."

But as in other investigations in the Sacramento, Ventura and Santa Barbara areas, cops hit a brick wall trying to determine the motive behind the murders.

For starters, if the killer was intent on rape alone, why strike when Keith Harrington was home? And there was nothing in their pasts that would indicate either Keith or Patrice would be targeted for death. No murder weapon was found at the scene, and the Orange County Sheriff's Department readily admitted they had few clues as to who and why.

"This one is a real mystery to us right now," one investigator told the *Los Angeles Times*.

And weirdly, life in Dana Point went back to normal for most people. Residents assumed that they were safe and not worried about a killer on the loose in their pristine corner of the world.

"We've had very few incidents at all that the police would consider a crime," a spokesperson for the homeowners' association said sniffily. "This is tragic, but we're not anxious for a lot of publicity about it."

By now, cops were calling the mystery killer the Night Stalker, later renamed as the Original Night Stalker to make way for fellow serial murderer Richard Ramirez, the homicidal Satanist who began killing in Los Angeles almost four years after the Harrington murders.

Investigator Paul Holes told NPR that bringing the phantom who came and killed with impunity was a staggering challenge for police.

"Part of it is just understanding – the geographic spread was huge. You know, the moniker Golden State Killer is so apt because he really was moving around hundreds of miles between cases," Holes said.

And the suspect was not a low-rent monster. He was not stalking poorer neighbourhoods, Holes said. No, he had preferences for the kinds of places he would hunt.

"So that was informative. But also looking at the neighbourhoods where he's attacking, it helped inform me about his tactics on how he's approaching a particular house, how he's leaving that house, how he's prowling through a neighbourhood. Why is he choosing that certain … that type of neighbourhood?"

Holes added, "One of the most informative aspects that I saw as I was visiting these neighbourhoods was that he wasn't attacking in lower-income areas at all. He was often attacking in upper-middle to even what I would consider close to upper-class neighbourhoods."

For a long time, investigators in northern, central and southern California focused on what Holes called the "troll under the bridge offender".

That would be someone homeless, living on society's fringes, likely with a police record for some kind of sexual offence. Maybe even driving a white, rusty old van that has seen better days. Holes quickly changed his presumptions.

"And as I'm looking at these neighbourhoods, going, 'If somebody like that showed up in this type of neighbourhood, he would stand out,'" Holes said.

"And so that's when I started to get insight as to who my offender could be, going, 'He blends in with the people who live in these types of neighbourhoods.'"

It was the Harrington double homicide in Dana Point that tweaked Holes's re-evaluation.

"It's almost an oceanfront type of community," the retired investigator said. "But this was an upper-scale neighbourhood at the time. It still is today. It is gated. It has security guards that work the gate. It has roving security. And as I'm driving around this neighbourhood, the question is, 'Well, why here?' He's elevating his risk to attack here when he could have gone right across the street and attacked in a community that didn't have security."

As Holes considered his quarry, it became apparent that the "where" piece of the puzzle was directly and profoundly related to the Golden State Killer's modus operandi. Specifically, his predilection to "hunt".

"So now that starts to make me question, well, maybe he's attacking in this neighbourhood because he's already chosen these victims," Holes told NPR.

"Well, when did he choose these victims? That becomes kind of the driving question of that investigation. Did he choose these victims because he ran into them somewhere else? Who are these victims? Victimology is huge. You know, so it's now diving into who they are and where he potentially could have interacted with them and seen where they lived."

Where did he zero in on the victims? At the supermarket? On the street? One thing was certain: the murderer was not merely opportunistic. His attacks were planned, methodical, and quite possibly carefully planned over several weeks.

Then there would be the trial balloons in the areas where his potential victims resided. Prowling, stalking, testing windows and doors. Watching carefully who was coming and going from his future crime scene.

"So that is where now I'm starting to think, okay, now he's choosing victims from outside of … he's not just prowling neighbourhoods and attacking when he sees an opportunity," Holes explained.

"He's possibly choosing victims elsewhere or had an interaction where he made a decision they're going to become victims and then assesses where they live to make sure that he can actually accomplish the crime and get away with it."

One neighbour later reported she heard screaming in the early hours of the morning. The injuries inflicted upon Keith were one thing. Patrice's injuries revealed an unspeakable level of barbarism.

And apparently, nothing was taken from the home, even though in his previous guises, DeAngelo was a compulsive collector of souvenirs and trophies from his crime scenes. Only the suspected murder weapon was missing.

Joseph DeAngelo had once more transitioned. No more fun and games – rape, then the brutal finality of murder. And he was getting better at his homicidal hobby. He was taking fewer chances and getting more notices in the newspapers for his barbaric crimes.

Even at this early date, he was no doubt seeing stories in the papers that, yes, the cops say some of these insidious murders could be linked.

Criminal profiler Leslie D'Ambrosia said the Original Night Stalker was perfecting his craft. He intended to make the murders appear to be burglaries that came off the rails. D'Ambrosia noted that in the Harrington double murder, he had removed the couple's bindings post-mortem.

But the killer's compulsions always revealed themselves. For example, Patrice Harrington was more savagely beaten than her husband. Joseph DeAngelo was not fooling homicide detectives with his botched burglary gambits.

Charlene Smith was also more brutally beaten than her husband, Lyman. She was also bitten, and so convincing cops it was an epic fail of a burglary wouldn't wash.

Roger Harrington suspected that the killer was someone from Patrice's past. Or maybe the pediatric nurse had stumbled on an illicit drug deal at the hospital where she worked.

The wealthy Roger hired a private investigator to do a deep dive into his daughter-in-law's history. There was a roommate that Patrice had left high and dry when Keith swept her off her feet and she moved in with him.

Ex-roommate Sandy Cook said the relationship had soured. Cook told the private eye that her estranged friend had two odd encounters. One was with a stranger when she was taking the garbage out. There was also a run-in with a jogger.

DeAngelo, in his various criminal incarnations, often posed as a jogger when he was on reconnaissance, trolling for his next victims. He frequently wore a jogging suit topped with a black toque.

For profiler D'Ambrosia, there was little doubt that the women were clearly the targets, the prize the killer coveted most. The slayings of the men were merely perfunctory. With the female victims, overkill was present at each and every crime scene.

D'Ambrosia believes the men were murdered before the woman was raped.

"Evidence reveals that the male victims were likely eliminated prior to the sexual assault and murder of the female victims," she wrote in her original psychological report.

"Keith Harrington was struck in the head with a blunt instrument. A crime scene assessment indicated that scratches and chipped wood on the headboard were likely made when he was struck in the head. A wood chip was discovered in the bed sheets between Patrice Harrington's legs. The location of the wood chip would support the theory that he was struck first. Because this happened in the Harrington case, it is likely that the offender struck and killed the male victims first in all the homicide cases."

Gags were never found at the crime scene, indicating that DeAngelo's first order of business after entering the home was to incapacitate the man. If he was dead, he could not call out.

That left time to repeatedly rape the female victim without fear of being interrupted. As an added touch, the female victims were discovered with marks and scratches around their mouths. Cops believe the murderer would slap or hit them in the minutes before he snuffed out their lives.

But then the question is why would he kill the man when his real quarry – the woman – might pass out, go into shock or vomit? The Golden State Killer's greatest thrill was instilling terror and fear into his victims. Why would he cheat himself out of that all-empowering sensation? But if the man was murdered in one room and the female target was in another, she might not know that her husband had just been butchered.

At one point, decades later, retired Orange County Sheriff's homicide investigator Larry Pool had a list of more than 8,000 suspects in the slayings south of Los Angeles. None of them were named Joseph James DeAngelo Jr.

Pool worked out of a small office at the Orange County Sheriff's headquarters in Santa Ana, working cold cases, trying to breathe life into the dead and long-forgotten cases.

One of the cases Pool often returned to was the unsolved August 1980 double murder of Patrice and Keith Harrington at the Niguel Shores home. The murders were ice cold after two decades.

The veteran homicide investigator spotted a notation in the file of the gruesome slayings from an earlier generation of detectives. It was a hunch and a beacon from the past.

Investigators in 1980 suspected that the Harrington murders could be chillingly linked to the killings of Lyman and Charlene Smith in Ventura County in March of that same year.

Keith Harrington's still-grieving brother, Brian Harrington, told Pool in 2004: "Look, it's not personal – I like you, but I don't want to talk to you again until you ID the offender."

On 25 April 2018, Pool picked up the phone and made the call.

11

Murder in Orange County

Manuela Witthuhn never really got used to living in America, even though she'd lived in the country since she was a child.

She had immigrated from Germany with her parents. And if she missed the old country, the great American homicide epidemic of the 1970s and 1980s was an incentive to return to Europe. Germany was safer and more relaxed than America during those days.

Southern California, in particular, became a sun-kissed graveyard with cops finding bodies all over the place. Residents were locking their doors, installing security systems and buying guns.

Murder was arriving with a thud in the suburbs of Los Angeles, including Irvine in Orange County, where Manuela lived quietly with her husband, David Witthuhn.

Irvine grew out of the miles of farms and citrus groves that dotted the area. Lima beans were also a big crop in the area.

It is what is described as a "master-planned city" and is considered part of the Los Angeles metropolitan area. Nearly always warm (only January and December see temperatures dip below 70°F [21°C]), Irvine's population exploded in the 50 years from 1970 to 2020.

The population went from 7,400 to more than 300,000 today, much of it driven by the technology and semiconductor sectors, with many of the corporations having their headquarters in Irvine. A robust academic sector has also helped drive growth.

Comic actor Will Ferrell was born and raised in Irvine. Other notable residents include slugger Mark McGwire and burlesque bombshell Dita Von Teese.

The predator had been watching Manuela. For how long, no one would ever know. Manuela Witthuhn was an attractive young blonde who lived with her husband, David, in a new development called Sycamore Park. She was described as an innocent in an increasingly debauched world.

It was almost six months after the brutal murders of Keith and Patrice Harrington in August 1980 in Dana Point, around 25 minutes southwest of Irvine.

For the Original Night Stalker, the neighbourhood with its young couples and many of the new homes was still sitting empty or unfinished. It was perfect for the Original Night Stalker.

6 February 1981 was unseasonably cold in Irvine. Few people were out and about, and no one noticed the stranger in their midst. He slipped through a side yard of an empty two-storey home and made his way inside.

Joseph DeAngelo knew the house was empty from his many scouting missions in the area. He was methodical in his approach to the business at hand, his hobby, his passion. Inside the empty house, he waited, looking for an opportunity to spy on the pretty blonde in the home the next yard over.

The Witthuhns lived in a modest 1,500-square-foot single-storey home typical of the development. The house, described by neighbours as "nice", had a half-atrium at its centre where two sliding glass doors opened, from the kitchen and a bedroom.

Manuela's parents, Horst and Ruth Rohrbeck, lived nearby.

On that February night, she was alone in the home. Her husband was in the hospital suffering from a viral infection. Being alone in the house made her nervous. It was an affliction her father had noticed, and he offered to leave his large German Shepherd with her for protection and company.

Manuela begged off. No, it's alright.

But she did have one bedtime quirk when she was alone. For some reason, she felt safer in a sleeping bag lying on top of the bed than in the bed itself.

A resident of a nearby home didn't realize that a prowler had romped into her home while she was out. The woman later realized she hadn't put on the deadbolt, which she always locked.

For the apex predator, he was now in the side yard of the house next door to the Witthuhns. And it was there that he waited for the lights to go out. And when they did, he slipped into her backyard and gently pried open the sliding doors with a screwdriver.

Finally, he pounced on her bed, put a screwdriver or knife to the terrified woman's neck and promised he would kill her if she made a sound. His promise would be written in blood.

The following morning, David called Manuela several times, but for some reason, she didn't pick up the phone. Worried, he called her parents, and her mother, Ruth, agreed to go round and check to make sure everything was fine.

What she discovered was something no parent should ever have to see. In the bedroom, Manuela was tucked into her sleeping bag. She had been bludgeoned to death in a frenzy of rage.

Although his body count was climbing, the Original Night Stalker was making mistakes. His efforts and staging of the crime scene to resemble a burglary gone awry were amateurish. It was clear that he wasn't a burglar whose nocturnal prowling had accidentally ended with homicide after he was caught in the act.

In the Witthuhn murder, the culprit had carried the couple's TV set to the back fence and just left it there. Again, knick-knacks and items of little value had been lifted. More valuable items like jewellery remained untouched.

Detectives at first wondered whether Manuela had woken up and surprised the burglar, provoking him to kill and then flee without his loot. They quickly dismissed that theory for several reasons. As was his standard MO, he had bound the victim. There were bruise marks from ligatures on her wrists, along with one of her ankles. But there were no ligatures left at the scene; the creeper had taken those with him. But why?

Why snatch a small bedroom TV and leave it by the fence? No, this was not a burglary. It was a sexually driven murder.

Manuela had been violently raped, likely many times. An autopsy revealed a bruise on her buttocks that was as though she had been punched there. In addition, there were the tell-tale marks or scratches around the area of her mouth.

It was not clear whether she had been slapped (a DeAngelo trademark) or had been gagged and no gag had been left at the murder scene. In the estimation of homicide detectives, the purpose of the invasion and defilement of Manuela had been murder. Cops felt comfortable scratching burglary off the list as a possible motive.

In most homicide investigations, detectives look at the victim's inner circle and those closest to them out of the gate. In the tragic case of Manuela Witthuhn, the person cops looked long and hard at was her husband. While he had an alibi by being in the hospital, he could have hired someone else to perform the grisly task, some investigators reasoned.

David Witthuhn was devastated. Not only had his wife been murdered, but now investigators were hounding him, certain he was their killer. And a lot of other people in the community believed it too.

A pall was cast over his life that never really went away.

Eventually, David married a co-worker named Rhonda, who was sympathetic to his plight. Some in the community – and the cops – were suspicious when the couple were married not very long after Manuela's murder. It didn't seem respectful.

And there was a third wheel in the crushing vice David found himself entangled in: the Golden State Killer himself. Taking his beloved wife was not enough for the madman, who continued to taunt the distraught car salesman.

His new wife, Rhonda Witthuhn, was terrified she could be the next to die and that the killer might target her. There were the sinister phone calls, an anonymous whisper on the other end of the line.

"I'm going to kill you," Rhonda recalled to *LAist*. "I'd just scream at the phone and hang up."

Decades later, for Rhonda, that hissing voice from hell has never left, an evil earworm on repeat.

As expected, Rhonda and David struggled to put Manuela's gruesome murder in the past. It seemed to haunt their every waking moment, even when they were at work at the House of Imports dealership.

But Rhonda thought David was a good guy, and that's why she had grown fond of him. He was quick with a smile and always willing to help out, no matter who asked for it.

"He was one of the good guys," Rhonda said.

The day Manuela's body was discovered, the murder was the talk of the dealership. And it was sobering when homicide detectives arrived, took over an office and began summoning staff one at a time. What they wanted was for the staff to tell them all about David. Rhonda thought it was crazy.

"They had their fights and stuff, but he adored her," she told *The Orange County Register* in 2018.

Instead of fearing that her friend and co-worker could be a violent monster, Rhonda reached out. She invited him to call her day or night if he wanted to talk. She reasoned that his wife's death must have been devastating and that he might feel more comfortable talking with a woman.

On his first night back at the home where his dreams were extinguished, David picked up the phone and called Rhonda. He poured his heart out over the phone and told his friend he was struggling.

The bedroom where Manuela had been murdered was in the process of being reassembled and painted, with the most visible aspects of the slaying being washed away. A crime scene cleaning crew tried to eliminate the gore. David later told Rhonda that the walls and cathedral ceilings had been scraped clean of blood. Rhonda offered the young widower her couch to sleep on.

Soon, the pair became inseparable. Eventually, she moved into the home that David had shared with Manuela and the place where she died.

It turned out that the decision to cohabitate may not have been the most prudent. Soon, there were whispers at work and around the neighbourhood. David Witthuhn now looked suspicious to co-workers, neighbours, and most importantly, the cops.

"It probably didn't help that I came along so soon," Rhonda said. "Some of the people wondered if David had done it."

Everyone on their street bought a new alarm system. Neighbours were standoffish if not downright frosty. David eventually resigned from the auto dealership where they both worked. Rhonda realized she didn't belong there either.

The final straw came when Manuela's father, Horst, came in one day, and David's former boss pointed to her and said that Rhonda was "David's new woman". Rhonda fled the dealership sobbing.

Still, she had never been in doubt of David's innocence. And hovering in the background was the chilling reality that the anonymous nut harassing them over the telephone was probably the real killer.

The couple attempted to build a new life together, but the ghost of Manuela and the demons they triggered in David Witthuhn were too powerful. He did his best to shield her from the periodic police questioning he had to endure. The sessions with the cops went on for years.

Rhonda revealed that in 1986, investigators again broached the subject of Manuela's still-unsolved murder. They were also investigating the murder of Janelle Cruz. She was an Irvine woman who had been raped and murdered.

There were many similarities between the two murders, cops told David. Years later, the Cruz murder would be tied to the Golden State Killer.

"He really thought they were going to lock him up," Rhonda later said. "He was sad that somebody would think that of him."

David's coping mechanism was booze. But the rum he drank only provided him with a temporary respite from the living nightmare he found himself in. He tried to start a business, but that meant too much time alone for a man whose memories were eating him alive.

"He went off the deep end," Rhonda sadly said. "He literally drank everything we had away."

After a decade together, Rhonda had had enough. The strain was too great, too many ghosts, and she was watching the man she loved spiral down the drain. David had lost everything: Manuela, now Rhonda, his job, his business and his home.

"It destroyed him," she said in 2018. "David started to drink heavily because he didn't know how to handle the anger he was left with."

She added, "He was such a gentle soul. It was inconceivable to him that anybody could do what happened to Manuela to another human being. I just wish David were here to see that Manuela is finally getting justice. I think he would just cry."

Rhonda heard that at one point he was living on the street, but the one-time couple lost contact with one another.

Then, in 1997, Rhonda saw a story on the front page of *The Orange County Register*. David's picture accompanied a story reporting that DNA had connected a slew of California killings and had cleared him in the murder of his first wife.

"I was just glad they weren't going to come after him anymore," Rhonda said.

David died of natural causes in 2008, never knowing the identity of the now-named Golden State Killer. Even after his early death, the serial killer continued to elude detectives.

In 2000, David told *The Orange County Register* that after he was cleared in 1997, he slept without nightmares for the first time in years.

"I feel vindicated," he said. "If he's actually ever caught, I'd be the first to pull the switch."

If he had been home that fateful evening, David Witthuhn also likely would have been murdered.

"It changed my whole life," he said. "From my health to everything. I'm still single. I rarely date."

He said, "I've had a hard time stopping being mad at everyone. Plus, I would accuse everyone. And, I was a suspect."

While the pair sometimes argued, they were a happy young couple with their lives in front of them. After her death,

Witthuhn continued to live in their Irvine home for six years before finally deciding it was time to move on.

"There was just so much to deal with, with being considered a suspect and trying to stay mentally stable," David told the *Register*. "Back then, there were no victim support groups. A lot of times, I could have used something like that."

Like other survivors, David Witthuhn was plagued by what-ifs and could-have-beens until the day he died.

The slayings would remain a mystery for another decade after he died. But before that, David had taken to true crime message boards looking for answers. He would periodically write missives to the true crime tribe.

According to Rhonda, at the time of his death, he was living in Big Bear, two hours and a world away from Irvine. But he had never stopped looking for the psycho who murdered Manuela and delighted in tormenting him.

He had been the prime suspect in the murder of his wife and Janelle Cruz five years later. David was grateful to be vindicated, but he remained a broken man.

When the Golden State Killer was finally arrested in 2018, Rhonda thought of her kind former husband and the torment he had endured. He, too, was a victim of the killer, and so was she.

She wrote on Facebook: "OMG it's over. They caught Manuela Witthuhn's serial killer. I so wish David were here to see justice."

The arrest also ended nearly four decades of fear for Rhonda as well. The killer's phone calls had been seared into her consciousness. Her fears ebbed away.

"He wouldn't come look for me," she added.

David's brother, Drew Witthuhn, said later in his victim impact statement that the murder of Manuela Witthuhn at the couple's new house in Irvine was a death sentence for David.

His executioner was Joseph James DeAngelo.

In his statement, Drew wrote:

After February 1981, my brother David lived, in my opinion, the next 27 years on borrowed time, from illness, despair, grief, anxiety, and depression, which took an accumulative toll that in 2008 finally became too much for his physical body to continue to endure. Those of us who spent time and lived with him saw and experienced a steady decline of faculties initiated in no small part by the convict's inhuman selection of his wife Manuela to remove him from. Dave went on with whatever strength he could muster and display, all the while knowing there would no longer be anniversaries or the anticipation of children, grandchildren, birthdays, vacations, family holidays together or anything remotely familiar to a normal life, as the convict made sure that in one instant those rights and certainties and so much more would be stolen from them both.

But for the Golden State Killer, there was still much more to take after the February 1981 murder of Manuela Witthuhn.

He would return to familiar territory a little less than six months later.

The results would be horrifically the same.

12

Familiar Hunting Ground

There was nothing to steal at Cheri Domingo's temporary abode, so she breathed easily. Too easily, as it would tragically turn out.

Nearly six months had passed since the Golden State Killer had last struck. On 6 February 1981, the heartless villain had raped and murdered Manuela Witthuhn, 28, in Irvine.

That was around 145 miles (233 km) south in Orange County.

Detectives had yet to make an arrest. They had persons of interest, namely, the dead woman's devastated husband, David Witthuhn.

In the hamlet of Goleta in Santa Barbara, the nightmare was still fresh from the brutal double murder of Dr Robert Offerman, a 44-year-old orthopedic surgeon, and psychologist Dr Debra Alexandria Manning, 35. As stated previously the pair were discovered shot to death on 30 December 1979, in the bedroom of Offerman's condominium. In addition, Manning had been raped.

Cops had initially pegged it as a botched burglary that ended in violence. No theories were suggested that the person responsible for the murders at the condo may be a serial killer.

Cheri Domingo was a dead ringer for tragic movie star Natalie Wood, who drowned off Santa Catalina Island in 1981. Cheri, a 35-year-old brunette beauty, was temporarily residing in a home in Goleta on Toltec Way. Domingo's late aunt had owned the house in the 400 block, and it was being sold. In the interim, Cheri was house sitting. The residence was several blocks south of the condo where Offerman and Manning had been murdered.

On 27 July 1981, Domingo and her 27-year-old former boyfriend, Gregory Sanchez, would become the tenth and eleventh victims of the Original Night Stalker, or as he came to be known, the Golden State Killer.

And if she was worried about the terrifying events in the neighbourhood from two years prior, she didn't show it.

Domingo had recently been laid off from her job at Trimm, a company that manufactured computer furniture. Now, armed with a load of contacts, she was looking for a job. She was not without opportunities. One of her options was to become a computer technology consultant.

On that warm, breezy summer evening in 1981, Domingo's former boyfriend, Greg Sanchez, was visiting. A large, handsome man with a 1970s-style moustache, he had pulled the plug on their relationship several months prior, but the pair remained close friends. And Cheri's two children loved him.

The house was located on a cul-de-sac where everyone typically knows everyone else's business. Theoretically, those easy sightlines should discourage any would-be thieves, prowlers, rapists or killers.

A neighbour told detectives the next day that she had heard a voice in the dead of night. It was a woman, sounding like she was trying to reason with someone. Her voice was controlled. The speaker was unemotional. The neighbour thought she heard the woman tell the stranger, "Take it easy." And then there was an eerie silence, but the busybody brushed it off.

She had likely just heard the final words ever uttered by Cheri Domingo.

"She pissed him off," a detective later said, interpreting what had happened.

A realtor, who had a scheduled showing, made the grisly discovery around noon. She called the listing agent and reportedly said, "I don't know what to say, but there is the body of a man face down in the bedroom."

The bodies of Cheri Domingo and Gregory Sanchez were found on the morning of 27 July 1981. He had been shot in the face, and there were also multiple blunt force trauma wounds on his head. Domingo was lying face down on the bed, nude and, again, covered with bedding. There were ligature marks on her wrists and ankles.

Her injuries were much worse. Again, the cause was blunt force trauma. In the tool shed in the backyard, investigators found the outline in dust of what appeared to be a crowbar. That was the likely murder weapon.

"My mom was my best friend growing up. She was only 19 when I was born, so when we'd go out to eat, she'd order a glass of wine with dinner, and the waiter would ask her for her ID," Domingo's daughter Debbi told *Good Housekeeping* in 2018. "She'd blush, and I'd bust out laughing, like, 'Come on, that's my mom!'"

When Debbi was 12, her parents divorced, with her father decamping to San Diego while Cheri stayed in Santa Barbara. Debbi said she and her brother alternated between their parents' homes.

"She went to work for a computer firm, where she met Greg Sanchez. They dated on and off again for years. He was about seven years younger than my mom, but they were very much in love. And I, of course, thought he was handsome and charming," Debbi said.

More than a few detectives suspected that a scraping sound the bedroom door made against the shag carpet may have alerted Sanchez that there was an intruder in the house. That was bolstered by physical evidence that he may have fought the killer.

Did Sanchez realize the phantom he was dealing with was the man responsible for the Offerman–Manning murders? Perhaps he tried to fight it out rather than be tied up and face certain death.

Sanchez's head had been covered with clothes pulled from the closet. Domingo had been raped, and ligature marks on her wrists and ankles suggested that she had probably been tied up. However, whatever was used to restrain her was missing.

Investigators did find a piece of shipping twine located near the bed where she died. And oddly, there were fibres from an unknown source scattered on her body.

One of the neighbours heard a gunshot around 3:45 a.m., followed by a symphony of barking dogs. They did not think to call the police.

Into this nightmare came Cheri Domingo's teenage daughter, Debbi.

"When I saw the yellow tape, I knew something was wrong. It was mid-afternoon on July 27, 1981, and I was 15 years old. My mom's best friend had just called the movie theatre where I worked," Debbi Domingo said.

"'Thank God, you need to come home,' she said, desperately. 'Debbi, you don't understand.' As I got in the car, I thought to myself, What's so darn important?

"When we turned the corner onto our street, I saw the bright caution ribbon wrapped around our house: Oh, that's what's so important.

"Several police vehicles were parked in the cul-de-sac as news crews and gawking neighbours stood across the street. I was scared, but I wasn't sure what of," she said.

Her first instinct was to see her mother.

"I want to go inside my house. When can I go into the house?" she asked a police officer.

He said, "You can't; it's too messy."

She recalled in 2018, "After what seemed like forever, I was finally told two dead bodies had been found, but they hadn't been identified yet. I put two and two together: If there's two bodies in our house, it's my mom and her boyfriend, Greg."

Detectives began trying to unravel how the latest shocking double murder had unfolded. The quiet area had been struck 18 months earlier, and suburbia had become the primary hunting grounds for the Golden State Killer.

A maze of streets, cul-de-sacs and easy-to-access backyards made the Goleta area ideal. Not only that, the area was flavoured with green spaces, parks, parkettes and trails. Most importantly, there was the San Jose Creek, so close to Offerman's condo on Queen Ann. Toltec Way, the scene of the latest crime, was just a hop, skip and jump away.

Part of the killer's MO was a studious approach to homicide. No doubt, he had spent weeks planning the kill, driving around, strolling in his jogging outfit unseen and unnoticed by the oblivious and dangerously naive suburbanites.

In addition to the autumn 1979 attempted murder and the Offerman double murder in December, another incident was also suspected to be the killer's handiwork. In September 1979, a young man was walking his dog off leash, and the curious canine wandered into a yard.

When the animal emerged, it was badly cut up. The dog walker rapped on the door, but there was no one home. Another neighbour called for help, and a friend picked up the man and his injured dog in a car. It took 70 stitches at the veterinarian to patch up the poor pup.

One resident in the area told detectives that on the evening of 26 July, they had seen a white male leaning against a tree. Around 10 p.m., another man and his wife went for an evening walk on that sultry summer evening. They claimed they had been followed by a white man in his thirties with blond, shoulder-length hair accompanied by a German Shepherd.

Then, at 11 p.m., a mother and her daughter were jogging when they saw a male matching the description of the stranger in the two previous incidents. He was on the sidewalk in front of the home whose backyard abutted the home where Cheri Domingo was staying.

Cops said the killer had entered the home through a small bathroom window. He then reached in and unbolted the door that led to the patio.

Now, detectives had a bloody mess on their hands. The bullet did not kill Greg Sanchez; it was being smashed 24 times in the head with a crowbar that did it. The bullet struck him while he was kneeling. Cops theorized he had gotten up after being shot, then charged the assailant.

And then he was bludgeoned with the crowbar.

The naked body of Cheri Domingo had been hogtied (hands and feet tied together). This double murder was overkill.

Santa Barbara sheriff's detectives quickly suspected that the same psychopath responsible for the Manning–Offerman murders was their guy in the Sanchez–Domingo homicides. He was also maybe the guy in those gruesome murders further south in Irvine, Ventura and Dana Point.

But investigators struggled to piece together a timeline.

The killer typically made his female victim restrain her paramour before she would be bound. Next, he would tie up the female and then the man's ankles. In the latest Goleta murders, there was no evidence that Sanchez had been bound.

He would then take the woman into another room and rape her repeatedly. The man was more likely to be left alone until the killer had completed his sickening sexual fantasies.

There is no doubt that the intruder had murder in mind when he entered Cheri Domingo's temporary home. But police suspected that his long-planned adventure in death did not go as planned.

The killer was fuelled by the fear of his victims; it was his elixir, his rocket fuel. Cheri Domingo was calm, and if the words attributed to her are true, she essentially told the man who had invaded her residence to get lost.

Greg Sanchez fought back. The Golden State Killer was also not used to that.

There was something frantic about the crime scene. And some aspects did not make sense. No doubt, the murderer reacted quickly when he shot Sanchez, but why did he not bind him?

And why did he hogtie Domingo? It's a practice that takes time. Why would the suspect do this when he had already fired a gun, shooting Sanchez, which may have alerted a neighbourhood busybody to call the cops?

It appeared as though the serial killer was getting sloppy and impetuous.

And where did he hone in on Cheri Domingo as a possible victim? Cops believed he may have worked as a painter or had a maintenance job at the Calle Real Shopping Center, a local mall.

Detectives suspected that the missing crowbar was the murder weapon, but it was nowhere to be found. Nor was the gun. Nothing had been stolen, and the house had not been ransacked.

And who was the young blond man with the German Shepherd? Cops noted that three-toed dog pawprints had been found outside at the Offerman crime scene. Could there be a connection?

It later emerged that the young man was the dog walker whose pet had been stabbed in the backyard of an empty home near Cheri Domingo's. There had been several dog murders earlier in the killer's CV during his rampage as the Visalia Ransacker.

Like the others, the murders of Domingo and Sanchez would take decades to solve.

But in every homicide, there are survivors like Domingo's daughter Debbi – just a teenager at the time her beloved mother was murdered. The murder has stained her life, coupled once more with chilling what-ifs.

"If I was there that night, I probably would have been murdered, too," she told *Good Housekeeping*.

While Cheri Domingo was young and gorgeous, it didn't stop her daughter from, well, acting like a teenager.

"By the time I turned 13 or 14, I started getting rebellious. I would break curfew and be up late talking on the phone when I should have been sleeping," she said. "I started smoking cigarettes and dating boys my mom would never have approved of. By the time I finished my sophomore year of high school, I was longing to do my own thing. We'd argue over stupid stuff. There were times I'd storm out of the house and stay with friends for a couple of days."

Their final conversation was a bitter affair between a headstrong daughter and a loving mother setting boundaries. Not out of spite, but love and concern. It was something Debbi discovered too late.

"That final conversation haunted me for years," she said. "On one occasion, I'd been gone for about three weeks, staying with a girlfriend 10 miles [16 km] away, and I realized I'd left my favourite bathing suit at home. I called her on Sunday, July 26, 1981, the day before she was killed, and said, 'When can I get my bathing suit?' She said, 'If you don't live here, then you forfeited everything that you left.'

"'Why don't you just stay out of my life!' I shouted, and hung up.

"Those were the last words I ever spoke to her. That final conversation haunted me for years. The guilt has been overwhelming at times, but now I know she knows I loved her and I didn't intend to leave things that way."

She was shocked, horrified and heartbroken. She was struck by the frenzied brutality of the murders of her mother and Greg.

"My mom's best friend's husband was the one who identified mom's body, and I later found out it took him a long time to do so because of the nature of the killing," she said. "At that time, nobody suspected it was a serial killer. Our neighbourhood was safe: no car accidents, no robberies. I mean, nothing.

"I spent hours talking to police. They asked me about mom's habits and the people she knew. Did she have any jealous ex-boyfriends? Any enemies at work? Did she sell drugs? Dad was questioned extensively. They sat him down in the master bedroom and grilled him to get a confession, but his alibi checked out."

Cops were not coming up with any possible motives or leads. It was likely the same killer had murdered Offerman and Manning, but there was no rhyme or reason for the bloodbath.

For Debbi Domingo, the murders were the central event of her young life. The house was packed, and there was a funeral to get through. Afterwards, the teen and her brother moved to San Diego to live with her father, stepmother and her two stepbrothers.

San Diego is four hours south of Goleta, but it might just as well have been around the corner. Debbi Domingo continued to be haunted by nightmares.

"In the first few years that followed, I'd have dreams where I was home and asleep in my bed the night of the murder. In this dream, I could hear the killer breaking in, and I could hear a scuffle going on, and I could hear my mom scream," she recalled.

"But I was able to pick up the phone and call the police, and they came and saved the day. In my dream, everybody lived happily ever after. I'd wake up from that dream, thinking, Ugh, Debbi. You screwed up. You should have patched things up with your mom, and you should have been home where you belonged, because everything would have been fine."

The years that followed were soured by the grisly events of July 1981. Debbi remained emotionally tormented, and that took a heavy toll to the point where she felt her life was broken and she lost touch with her late mother's side of her family.

"I shut everything out, and it stayed that way for about 20 years. After finishing high school, I eventually started my own family," Debbi said. "I developed depression and drug addiction issues. It kept getting worse and worse until, basically, I hit rock bottom. I was a single mother with multiple children in foster care. I was homeless and addicted to drugs. I was hopeless."

Having lost her children, who were living with her brother and his wife, there was nowhere to go but up. Her brother asked to come over on a Saturday, have some dinner and stay overnight. Then, brother and sister would go to church on Sunday morning.

It was an eye-opening and ultimately redemptive experience.

"Going to church was hard. I'd sunk so low, and my self-worth was non-existent. It was humiliating, so I sat in the back row and I tried to be invisible. But then something miraculous happened. The pastor kept quoting this verse: 'Come to me, all you who are weary, and I will give you rest for your souls, for my yoke is easy and my burden is light.' I felt like God was whispering in my ear over and over again, 'I want to carry your burden.' I was so moved and so humbled."

That Sunday morning sermon would be the turning point for the young woman who had been broken into a million pieces by murder. Her life started getting better. Debbi became more self-disciplined and found a job.

And, most importantly, she regained custody of her children.

Like David Witthuhn, Debbi Domingo was another casualty of the Golden State Killer. Witthuhn never had the chance to see his wife Manuela's killer arrested, convicted and jailed forever. His consolation was DNA clearing him of any involvement in Manuela's 1981 slaying in Irvine.

Debbi was much luckier. Today she is married, has good relationships with her children, grandchildren and extended family, and she works in corrections. She has rebuilt the tattered relations with her mother's family.

Even with the many good things in her life, Cheri Domingo – and the cruel fate that befell her – continued to hover in Debbi's aura. The good and the bad.

More than 20 years had passed, and her mother's case had remained cold. Forgotten by most but not all. Debbi remembered, and so did the detectives. Debbi hadn't spoken to the investigators for years.

"But in 2002, I got a call from the Santa Barbara Sheriff's office saying they were actively investigating Mom's case again. The department believed the killing was related to a series of murders and rapes," Debbi said. "I was shocked.

"My life had been so impacted by the wreckage of what the murderer left behind, but I'd finally been able to move on into a normal life."

Detectives gave her the lay of the land: The murders of Cheri Domingo and Greg Sanchez were likely linked to a series of rapes and murders that had inflicted monstrous pain from one end of the state to the other. He was the Visalia Ransacker, the East Area Rapist and the Original Night Stalker.

"About 10 years later, forensic experts extracted DNA samples that officially proved Mom and Greg were murdered by him," Debbi said.

"I'm 20.5 years sober right now, have a great family, and I feel incredibly blessed. The only thing that was missing? A lack of closure in my mom's case."

She added, "Have police finally caught the Golden State Killer? He'd be in his 60s or 70s today and I used to picture him shopping in a grocery store or driving on a freeway or coaching a baseball team, or he's sitting on a front porch drinking iced tea.

"For years, he's gone to great lengths to stay undetected, but we need to find him. I'm ready for peace."

Under the photo of Greg Sanchez in his high school yearbook, he prophetically wrote: "Even lucky men die."

And then the Golden State Killer went radio silent. There were no new rapes or murders that could be traced to him after the terrible murders of Cheri Domingo and Sanchez.

Suddenly, he just stopped.

But before the coda was written on his killing career, there would be one last hurrah.

13

The Final Act

The killer had left bodies scattered from Sacramento to Dana Point, along with dozens of rapes and other insidious crimes.

As detailed previously, his last bloodletting had been on 27 July 1981 in Goleta in Santa Barbara County. The victims were Cheri Domingo, 35, and her 27-year-old former boyfriend, Gregory Sanchez. The pair had been bludgeoned in Cheri's late aunt's home.

It had been the serial killer's second visit to Goleta. In 1979, he had murdered a doctor and his girlfriend in a condo just blocks away from the July 1981 homicides.

But then he simply stopped.

The public tends to believe that a serial killer's bloodlust can never be sated until they are captured and put behind bars. But these bogeymen of the late twentieth century have frequently been very elusive, difficult to identify and to capture.

Most don't fit the tropes of the serial killer from central casting. Often, they are employed, married with children and can be perfectly pleasant neighbours. And just like those of us who aren't plagued by homicidal urges, even for serial killers, sometimes life gets in the way.

But studies have revealed that the desire to murder other human beings can come and go. BTK Killer Dennis Rader managed to put his compulsions on ice and give up the killing game. He murdered at least ten people between 1984 and 1991.

During that time, he took a five-year break from terrorizing Wichita, Kansas. After strangling Vicki Lynn Wegerle, 28, on 16 September 1986, with a nylon stocking, Rader stopped killing for five years. Dolores Earline Johnson Davis, 62, was his comeback killing on 19 January 1991.

Rader later explained the break, saying he had young children at the time and family life made his murder excursions difficult to arrange. And he was getting older.

"It seemed like as I got older, I started making … well, physically, I just wasn't up to it," Rader told *Dateline NBC* following his capture. "I knew if I'd have to fight with somebody, it would have to be an older person because I'd be just winded or wouldn't be able to fight physically."

Golden State Killer Joseph James DeAngelo Jr also took a five-year sabbatical. After the 1981 Goleta murders, he went quiet; not even a peeper or prowler was linked to him.

In 2007, the FBI produced a report that tried to bring some rigour to the question: Why do serial killers stop killing?

Researchers said changing life circumstances can make murder more risky and difficult. Or, less appealing to the apex predator. The report cited "increased participation in family activities, sexual substitution and other diversions".

University of Pennsylvania lecturer Mark Safarik, a former member of the FBI's Behavioral Analysis Unit, noted that the change in circumstances doesn't need to be a major life event. It could be something as simple as changing jobs or working the overnight shift, primetime for a killer. That eliminates the stalking portion of the equation, making targets harder to identify.

A new relationship could also derail the dormant killer's nocturnal ambitions.

After murdering a college professor in Michigan in 1986, Jeffrey Gorton waited five years to notch his second kill, a flight attendant he raped and murdered. The FBI noted that during the five years Gorton abstained from homicidal violence, he was married and "engaged in cross-dressing and masturbatory activities, as well as consensual sex with his wife in the interim". The aforementioned activities served as a substitute for killing.

And as time goes on, the once brazen killers become increasingly paranoid that they are going to get caught, the report suggested.

Safarik said, "Jeffrey Dahmer became afraid that police were going to identify him on a number of occasions, so he would stop for a period of time."

Joseph DeAngelo Jr was 41 years old when his murder spree concluded. Research shows that serial killers eventually age out of murder. It becomes too difficult physically.

The exception is Toronto serial killer Bruce McArthur, who was 66 when he was arrested in 2018 and was still hunting for victims in the Canadian city's gay village. Evidence revealed that the shopping mall Santa Claus didn't start his reign of terror until he was 59 years old. Between 2010 and 2017, a total of eight men disappeared from the LGBTQ district. He pleaded guilty in 2019 to eight counts of first-degree murder.

Now, it had been almost five years since DeAngelo had struck. What did he do during that time? Were there unknown victims, or did he simply give himself a respite, a chance to recharge his batteries?

The year 1986 would see his finale. Whether the Golden State Killer knew it at the time is unknown. He has never said, and really, neither have the cops. No one knows why he put his rampage on pause.

In the five years since the Domingo murders, the world had changed. Music video channel MTV debuted in August 1981, with the days of disco ending with a whimper and giving way to punk and new wave. Well-coiffed British group the Pet Shop Boys, with their hit "West End Girls", were number one on the Billboard Hot 100.

NBC's triumvirate of sitcoms, *The Cosby Show*, *Family Ties* and *Cheers*, owned the airwaves that year, while Ridley Scott's dark fantasy *Legend*, starring Tom Cruise, Tim Curry and Billy Barty, was the box office champ in late April and early May.

In the White House, Ronald Reagan was enjoying his second term as US president as the embers of the Cold War were fading to smoke.

And Janelle Lisa Cruz was a typical 1980s teenager. Her family described the 18-year-old Irvine woman as a "poet and a warrior".

"A representation of all that is good in the world. She was a young woman who was struck down well before her time. But first, to us, she was just Janelle," her family later wrote in her obituary. "Her sense of life, fun and humour was infectious. The kind of girl who, if she laughed, you laughed. And if she smiled, your heart just soared knowing she thought well of you."

The teenager was close with her family and had an affinity for screen goddess Marilyn Monroe. She graduated from high school and was looking forward to a bright future. Her turbulent teen years hadn't always been easy. The Mariel Hemingway lookalike had taken to cutting herself during this time, landing in the psychiatric wards of two different hospitals.

That was now in the past. She had completed a ten-month stint in the US Job Corps in Utah, which she enjoyed immensely. Janelle returned to Irvine, where she made spending money working as a part-time cashier at Bullwinkle's Pizza.

On Sunday, 4 May 1986, a male friend visited Janelle at the family home. They were in her bedroom when they thought they heard a noise outside. The pair scoured the yard but didn't see anything. They concluded the noise was probably a cat prowling the neighbourhood.

Around 10:45 p.m., about 15 minutes after Janelle and her friend heard the first mysterious noise, they heard another. This time it was coming from the garage. She thought it was likely the washing machine. This explanation wasn't good enough for her male friend. He was creeped out and decided to leave.

The sounds Cruz heard and dismissed were probably from her killer, stumbling around in the dark, Orange County District Attorney investigator Erika Hutchcraft told CBS News.

"We know he's a peeper, we know he's a prowler, and he likes to watch people," Hutchcraft said. "So we know he was probably watching her with her friend, and then he was able to watch the male friend leave, so he knew that she was alone."

Police believe Janelle had slipped out to get a few things. One neighbour said they heard her Chevette with the distinctively loud muffler (silencer) return home around 11:15 p.m. As the neighbour heard just one door on the Chevette close, she assumed Janelle was alone.

In a chilling replay of the Domingo–Sanchez murders five years earlier, it was a real estate agent who had a scheduled showing at the home who found Janelle's body at around 5 p.m.

She had been raped and beaten beyond recognition, her teeth found in her hair and lungs. Her stepfather later reported that his pipe wrench was missing. Cops deemed the wrench the likely murder weapon.

Most of the battering she had endured was around her forehead.

Janelle had one unfortunate habit that may have led to her death: she often forgot to lock the doors to the family home. For an experienced prowler like the Golden State Killer, that was like manna from heaven.

Investigators theorized that her killer surprised Janelle in the kitchen, battering her on the forehead. Evidence pointed to a struggle; the teenager had valiantly fought back against the intruder, as evidenced by the blood at the scene. Naturally, she tried to get away as there was more blood on the inside of the front door. Detectives found more blood on the headboard of her bed.

Her nude body was placed diagonally across her bed with her bra pulled down to her waist. And, as per the killer's MO, her bloody head was covered with blankets.

Janelle had also been violently raped. Forensic investigators found lint near her body. It was medium blue and likely from a bath towel that had been torn and used to gag the terrified teen. Again, the gag was missing. There were also abrasions on her wrists.

Detectives theorized that the kitchen attack likely left Janelle incapacitated, making the killer's despicable next steps easier. Police found blades of grass near her head, and the tell-tale tennis shoe prints were discovered on the east side of the suburban home.

At the time of the murder, the victim's 17-year-old sister, Michelle, was vacationing in Mammoth Mountain in the Sierra Nevada, about 340 miles (550 km) north. When a friend called to tell the teen about her sister's murder, Michelle at first misheard what she was being told.

She asked the caller, "Janelle was married?!"

The mistake may have been rooted in the long white dress and shawl the girls' mother had recently purchased for Janelle on a family trip to Palm Springs. Janelle had dreamed of getting married someday, and the teen had a new, positive outlook.

Her mother, Diane Stein, told filmmaker Cameron Cloutier that it was a far cry from her difficult early teenage years.

"Life," Stein said, "was going to happen again."

Now, the family was left with just memories. How much fun did they have on that Palm Springs trip? Stein said they laughed, they shopped, and Janelle modelled the dress she adored. That led to discussions of her marriage and wedding day sometime in the future.

Stein said, "We buried her in that white dress."

Friends who Janelle best disputed some of the post-mortem slut-shaming that was directed at the dead girl. She was a friendly, popular girl who had a bubbly personality. Boys liked her. End of story. She was a Southern California girl of her time.

People whose lives have never been touched by homicide are oblivious to the generations of pain such a crime unleashes on a family unit. And if the case goes cold? That makes it much worse.

Janelle's family was devastated by the murder, and it changed their lives forever.

"Our family unit had been shattered," her sister Michelle Cruz told Oxygen.com, adding that the tight-knit family abandoned their home in the wake of the tragedy.

"We never went back to that house. We sold it," Michelle said, noting that the home was an eternal reminder of the horrors her sister had endured.

After the murder, the family relocated to Florida, where they still live.

"My daughter must have been a very brave girl at that moment, and she probably fought him off," Stein told First Coast News in 2018. "I left for vacation and gave her a kiss goodbye."

Bitterly, it was the first time Janelle had been left alone overnight.

"This is one of the situations when they call you in the middle of the night, midnight, and give you the news that your daughter has just been murdered," Stein added.

"The first thing you think of is, 'I want to go home and help my daughter,' but she's not alive, but that's the first thing a mother thinks, 'Oh I want to go home real quick and help her' … but, you can't."

Stein added, "I cried on the airplane. Everybody on the airplane felt bad for me, and my little son was running through the aisles. My husband finally held him, but yeah, I cried all the way home."

The heartbroken mom believes the killer had been stalking her daughter for weeks. There were the mysterious phone calls, for starters. Innocent at the time; something very sinister now.

"He would say, 'I'm going to kill you,' in a low but almost childish voice on the phone. We thought he did it in a child's voice, someone was just fooling around," Stein explained, adding she only learned later it was all part of the Golden State Killer's MO.

"He looks in through the windows," Stein said. "He usually watches people for a little while before he goes to the house."

Stein said she avoided the grisly details for years. She knows enough about Janelle's last hours.

"The one question I'd like to ask him is, why did he pick our house? Why? Go figure," Stein said.

"I guess this is every mother's idea of sadness, just very sad, she was just a beautiful girl, she was robbed of her life and we were robbed of loving her and having her, but she still lives, she lives in the story."

One of the reasons Janelle was targeted was the location of the family home. The Cruz home was only 1.7 miles (2.7 km) from the victim Manuela Witthuhn's house. No doubt the killer was familiar with the area, had cruised, peeped, stalked and scouted for victims.

Criminal profiler Leslie D'Ambrosia believes that Irvine was a "comfort zone".

In many ways, it was. It was the site of the Witthuhn murder in 1981. But California in general – and Southern California in particular – is an endless sea of ideal hunting grounds for a killer with Joseph DeAngelo's MO: suburban, close to creeks, trails, and freeways.

Still, during his five years of inactivity, the Los Angeles area offered a target-rich environment and ticked all of the Golden State Killer's boxes. But he never ventured into LA proper on a hunting expedition. Instead, he preferred places like Goleta (where he struck three times) and Irvine, close to the I-5 North.

What cops and the public didn't realize at the time was that Janelle Cruz would be the final victim. When more rapes and murders with his stamp failed to materialize, detectives suspected that he was either in jail or dead. Or was this monster in the military? Or did he simply move elsewhere?

But when did he put the coda on his homicidal career? It was an area he was familiar with and had struck before.

D'Ambrosia suspected that perhaps the serial murderer had been shot and killed by a homeowner during one of his homicidal expeditions or "adventures".

In 1986, there was suspicion among police detectives that the cases in Sacramento, Contra Costa County and the murders in Southern California were linked. But that was all they had: suspicions and a chillingly similar MO. Their quarry was clever and fairly careful.

DNA, databases and cooperation between various law enforcement agencies today would have quickly connected the crimes.

As we know now, it is not impossible or unheard of for a serial killer to suddenly stop murdering. And this is almost certainly what happened with Joseph James DeAngelo Jr. He just stopped.

DeAngelo, while not exactly an old-timer, was also not in the sweet bloom of youth.

D'Ambrosia theorized that the killer was based in the Ventura area, north of Los Angeles, because that's where the attacks began. The first kill for serial murderers is frequently closer to home.

Retired Contra Costa cold case investigator Paul Holes believed the killer simply aged out and was no longer capable of dominating his victims as he once had.

"I believe what ended up happening were two things: In 1981, he ends up going in to kill Gregory Sanchez and Cheri Domingo. And he gets in a physical fight with 6-foot-3 Gregory Sanchez. And I think that physical altercation with Sanchez scared him. We don't have an attack for five years," Holes told ABC News.

"But then … for some reason, he runs across beautiful 19-year-old Janelle Cruz and can't help himself. And kills her."

Holes added that he believed age was catching up with the killer.

"At this point, he's an aging offender," Holes said. "And so, he is no longer in that prime where he's not going out as frequently as he wants, naturally due to his age."

The famed homicide detective believes that although it is within the realm of possibility that the Golden State Killer continued his murderous ways undiscovered, he adds that it's "unlikely".

"But I can't say for sure," Holes said. "I know we have looked over the years for additional cases, 'cause we wanted to try to see if we could find more. And we haven't. So, it's not just starting that search now. That's been ongoing for a long time. And we've been unsuccessful."

By the end in May 1986, there had been a dozen murders, at least 50 rapes and countless home burglaries throughout California. The violent crime spree had begun ten years earlier with a burglary in Rancho Cordova, where the fiend robbed a woman of cash and jewellery.

Investigators believe the murders began when he was 31 years old and concluded when he was 40, at the time of the Janelle Cruz slaying.

But the Golden State Killer was unusual among serial murderers. Most do not take five-year-long sabbaticals. It is extremely rare. Only the BTK (Blind Torture Kill) Killer, Dennis Rader, has taken a significant amount of time off from murder and mayhem.

"Most of them don't have long cooling off periods between their killings that last for years," criminologist Dr Scott Bonn told Oxygen.com.

"Serial killing is almost like a drug addiction. It's a compulsion. They have to have it, and they do it again and again until they are caught or killed."

Bonn said the Golden State Killer and BTK were similar, adding that the latter was able to get through the murder-free years.

"In his case, he was able to sustain himself through auto-erotic fantasy," Bonn said. "He would relive his crimes in a way to control his urges without killing again, but that's unusual."

As for the Golden State Killer, he may have sustained himself by making prank calls to his victims for at least 15 years after the Janelle Cruz homicide.

"It would be a way of maintaining control, especially over these same people," Bonn explained. "There are different categories of serial killers, and there is a category called power-control killer, which is what BTK was, and I think this guy [Golden State Killer] has aspects of that. He had a law enforcement background. I think he was a control freak, and he was able to get a feeling of that same sense of intimidation and dominance without killing, through harassing phone calls. I think it probably gave him a fix of that adrenaline."

Bonn also pointed to the 1981 double murder of Cheri Domingo and Greg Sanchez, who valiantly fought back against the Golden State Killer. It probably scared him, Bonn noted.

"It's conceivable that he was intimidated and given pause by that encounter in 1981 and then by 1986, and his urge to kill became overwhelming enough he had to kill again," Bonn said, adding that by that time, DeAngelo was probably aging out.

"It's absolutely true that criminals tend to age out of crime especially if the crimes they commit are violent in nature, which of course rape and robbery and serial killing is," Bonn said. "Physically, he may not have been up to it anymore. I think that's a possibility."

During the period of the final two murders, DeAngelo also became a father to two baby girls. Having small children can impede even the most organized or indifferent parent. Did the killer reconsider his secret life of rape and murder because of parenthood or because his wife was pregnant?

And committing his vile crimes was not getting easier. There were the close calls, and having children may have convinced him to eventually stop.

Finally, there remains the possibility that the Golden State Killer took his macabre show on the road and murdered while he was on vacation.

Joseph James DeAngelo Jr had evaded police for more than a decade. In 1986, they were no closer to closing the homicide, rape and burglary cases.

He had been methodical, careful, and well-prepared for his brazen attacks.

In the 1980s, he likely would have scoffed at the notion that one day, modern technology would lead dogged investigators to his doorstep. It would take two decades, but eventually, he would be found.

14

Cold Case

The barbaric murder of Janelle Lisa Cruz on Sunday, 4 May 1986, was the Golden State Killer's grand finale.

He had come out of a five-year hibernation to again satisfy his bloodlust. And then he simply vanished back under the slimy rock from whence he emerged.

The heartless slaying of Cruz, 18, like the others, quickly went cold. After a few years, the evidence was boxed and put in storage in the hopes of a future miracle.

The evidence in the 11 other Golden State Killer case murders was destined to meet the same sad fate: a grey, concrete, temperature-controlled evidence room.

It would be 15 years before the investigations into the murders, rapes and myriad other crimes would see somewhat of a break. But for the time being, the maniac had effectively gotten away with it.

There were a lot of reasons the investigations stalled. A formidable foe was the era itself before databases, DNA, CCTV and myriad other modern investigation tools. The widespread locations of the rapes and murders also created difficulties.

Some of the detectives who worked on the investigations that stretched from the state capital in Sacramento to Dana Point in Orange County blamed "poor communication between agencies, investigative tunnel vision and antiquated technology".

And the killer was clever, resourceful and careful, and he left little behind in the way of evidence.

Descriptions of the man known variously as the Visalia Ransacker, the East Area Rapist and the Original Night Stalker varied widely. He was skinny, he was husky, he was young, he was old. There appeared to be no clear description.

What was known was his methodology, his preferred killing grounds and his violent nature.

"We were in the dark ages back then, especially compared to today," retired Sacramento County Sheriff's detective Richard Shelby told the *Los Angeles Times*.

Cops kept waiting for the magic bullet in the way of evidence or a wife, girlfriend or relative dropping a dime, but it never came.

"The Son of Sam got caught off a parking ticket," said Wendell Phillips, another former detective. "Sometimes you just have to get lucky. And in this particular case, all the luck went with him."

And the culprit was lucky right from the start. Visalia Police reached out to the Sacramento Sheriff's Office to give them a heads up that their Ransacker and the East Area Rapist may be the same guy. No one was interested, one former cop said.

Richard Shelby said when he scoured the Visalia cases much later, he noted the similarities, particularly the modus operandi. He, too, was met with a wall of indifference. And several detectives in varying jurisdictions suspected the rapist was a police officer.

Sacramento Sheriff's detectives and other members of the East Area Rapist task force were never informed that an Auburn cop named Joseph James DeAngelo Jr had been fired for shoplifting dog repellent and a hammer.

After the murders of Rancho Cordova couple Brian and Katie Maggiore on 2 February 1978, the East Area Rapist ceased operations. There were greener pastures with less heat.

In a bloody 20-month stretch, from the end of 1979 to August 1981, the Golden State Killer murdered nine people in Southern California. Even when a friendly investigator from another jurisdiction suggested a possible link, they were stonewalled.

In Orange County, investigators with the Sheriff's Department initially liked a guy named Greg Gonzalez for the Janelle Cruz murder. As in the slaying five years earlier of Manuela Witthuhn, who lived nearby, Janelle had been raped and beaten.

But Detective Larry Montgomery later said he could not link the slayings despite some obvious parallels.

Gonzalez had met Janelle in drug rehab and confessed to an informant that he had murdered her. Between the time Janelle had been murdered and the discovery of her body, Gonzalez had been arrested on suspicion of another rape.

"I wasn't looking for another suspect because it appeared to me to be Greg Gonzalez," Montgomery told the *Los Angeles Times*. "Therefore, there was nothing else to look for. I had a pretty darn good suspect. How often do they confess to it and attempt to do a similar crime two days before?"

But one year after Janelle's terrible death, prosecutors dropped the charges against Gonzalez, even though he confessed. Blood and semen tests would eventually clear him.

Montgomery said that at this point in 1987, he was now empty-handed. He never thought that the murderer he was after was a serial killer.

"In those days, we didn't have DNA," former Santa Barbara County detective Fred Ray said in 2018. "Other than ballistics, we had very little evidence from the scene that would connect all the cases."

The multitude of failed investigations was all plagued by the limitations of their time. Three decades into the future and the killer would have been behind bars or getting a lethal injection in the death house at San Quentin. But that was then.

Forensic criminologist and former San Jose detective Ron Martinelli outlined the cops' handicaps in the 1970s, 1980s and 1990s.

"We had no patterning, criminal psychological profiling or strict protocols for maintaining the integrity of a crime scene," he said. "It was just basically a lot of gumshoe and asking questions and trying to gather as much evidence as possible."

But every year after Janelle Cruz's 1986 murder, there were new advances in forensics and technology. Slowly but surely, science was catching up to the cops.

There were hundreds of suspects, but investigators focused on two other men besides Gonzalez.

Santa Barbara County investigators liked Goleta homeboy Brett Glasby. But before cops could have a chat with Glasby, he was murdered in Mexico in 1982. That ruled him out in the 1986 slaying of Janelle Cruz.

Also considered a potential suspect was high-ranking member of the racist prison gang, the Aryan Brotherhood, Paul "Cornfed" Schneider. He was residing in Orange County when the Harringtons, Manuela Witthuhn, and Janelle Cruz were murdered. The pall of suspicion was cast upon Schneider until the 1990s, when DNA definitively cleared him of any involvement in the slayings.

When Lyman Smith and his wife were murdered in 1982, for a time cops liked a guy called Joe Alsip, a one-time friend and business partner of the dead man. The men were at odds over business dealings, as discussed in a previous chapter.

Alsip's pastor told detectives that his parishioner spilled his guts about the slaying during a family-counselling session. He was arraigned for the murders in 1982, but the charges didn't hold up and were later dropped. DNA also confirmed his innocence in 1997.

But investigators were getting closer to the truth, even if it didn't appear that way, and they may not have been aware which direction the wind was blowing.

DNA was proving to be the magic bullet needed to close unsolved homicides.

In 2001, for the first time, DNA offered definitive answers on the maniac who had raped and murdered from one end of California to the other. The fetish freak known as the East Area Rapist and the Original Night Stalker were the same person. Some Sacramento Sheriff's detectives tried to link the murders in Goleta in Santa Barbara County to the same killer. It was the modus operandi and the fiend's tell that stood out.

Some detectives also suspected a connection, but gut instincts don't hold up in a court of law. Now, the science proved it.

That year, several rapes in Contra Costa County that cops believed were committed by the East Area Rapist were linked by DNA to the Smith, Harrington, Witthuhn, and Cruz murders. Ten years later, DNA indicated that the Domingo–Sanchez murders were also committed by the Golden State Killer.

"So when I open that file cabinet up and I'm seeing this red EAR and starting to flip through these files, I'm recognizing, oh, this is a serial rapist, and that EAR stood for East Area Rapist," retired Contra Costa investigator Paul Holes said.

"This is an offender that actually started up in Sacramento in mid-1976 and was attacking all over the east area of

Sacramento, Citrus Heights, Rancho Cordova, et cetera. So that's how this rapist got his moniker.

While the Golden State Killer's last known crime was in 1986 with the murder of Janelle Cruz in Orange County, the terror never left the victims. After all, as far as they knew, he was still out there, ready to emerge from his bleak cocoon to strike once again.

Many of the victims were unable to move on from the horrific tragedies that had befallen them. Burrowed in their consciousness was the chilling sense that they were not safe. They would never be safe.

"Oh, that was a huge fear for some of these victims," Holes recalled. "I had one woman who went to a vacation house. She had a cabin up in the foothills. And the thermostat was set different than what she remembered setting it when they had previously left. And she calls me. And it's nighttime. And she's saying, 'I think he's been here.' So she's constantly thinking that this guy is going to come back."

He added, "I had another woman who, after hearing about a potential suspect in Sacramento, and he was still out and about, she moved to Mexico. She wanted to get away because she thought he would come back. These victims – after he left, they continued to be traumatized by the thought that he was still out there. And the East Area Rapist played on that because he would call some of these victims, sometimes years later, to let them know he was still around."

Indeed. Almost from the start of the East Area Rapist's reign of terror, there were the taunts – and the sinister phone calls.

The first three calls were taunting missives to the Sacramento County Sheriff's Office in March 1977. They came in the late afternoon, and the caller told the dispatcher, "I'm the East Side Rapist." The calls were identical, each with the same message and the caller laughing, then hanging up.

In December 1977, he called the Sacramento Police Department with this taunt: "You're never gonna catch me, East Area Rapist, you dumb fuckers; I'm gonna fuck again tonight. Be careful!"

While the first three calls were not recorded, this one was, and cops released it to the public.

Later that month, the call rang again with two calls but one message: "I am going to hit tonight. Watt Avenue."

The call was again recorded, and the anonymous man on the other end of the line was identified as the same person who made the call earlier in the month. As promised, vigilant cops spotted a masked man on Watt Avenue around 2:30 a.m. The prowler gave them the slip after he was spotted riding a bike on the Watt Avenue Bridge.

He was again seen at 4:30 a.m. when he ditched the bike and fled the area.

The East Area Rapist's first victim was called on 2 January 1978. The caller asked for "Ray", but it was a wrong number, or so she thought. But later that evening, she received a threatening call. The woman later identified the voice as that of the rapist.

The caller snarled, "Gonna kill you … gonna kill you … gonna kill you … bitch … bitch … bitch … bitch … fuckin' whore."

The East Area Rapist also called a local counselling service on 6 January 1978. He told the operator that he was the East Area Rapist and told them, "I have a problem. I need help because I don't want to do this anymore."

The man and a counsellor spoke briefly before he said, "I believe you are tracing this call," and hung up.

One victim received a call at her place of work, a Denny's restaurant, in 1982. The caller threatened to rape her again. Holes said that it's likely the suspect spotted his victim at the diner and recognized her.

For years, David Witthuhn, the widower of murder victim Manuela Witthuhn, received the cruel phone calls. Making matters worse, Witthuhn himself lived for years under a cloud of suspicion until he was cleared in 1997.

The second-to-last known call came in 1991 when the suspected perpetrator rang one of his earlier victims, who spoke with him on the phone for about a minute. In the background, she heard a woman and children. Investigators suspected their suspect was a family man.

The final call came on 6 April 2001 – 15 years after the last murder. A story had appeared in *The Sacramento Bee* the day before that linked the East Area Rapist and the Original Night Stalker.

The caller asked his earlier victim, "Remember when we played?"

"He had tracked her down 24 years later," Paul Holes said.

It was Holes who began filling in the blanks on the mystery man in 1997.

"Well, I had a DNA profile from three cases in Contra Costa County. And talking with Lieutenant Larry Crompton, he pointed me down to Santa Barbara. And then, eventually, I'm now talking with the Orange County Sheriff's lab, who had a DNA profile from two homicides," Holes said.

"And in '97, we had different technologies. But I told that DNA analyst, I'm going to be coming back to you once I get caught up on my side with technology."

Holes explained that four years later, his lab caught up.

"And now I have updated DNA profiles that are then compared with those profiles down in Orange County, and they matched," he said.

"Now, in March of 2001, I knew that the East Area Rapist in Northern California was the guy that they knew as the Original Night Stalker, who had killed ten people between 1979 and 1986 after he had left Northern California."

For investigators across the state, the hunt for the perpetrator became an obsession. After the 2001 DNA revelation that they were looking for a single perp and the subsequent bump in publicity, the case again went quiet, forgotten by the public in the wake of the 9/11 2001 terrorist attacks on New York City and Washington and the War on Terror.

But there was also a growing contingent of true crime enthusiasts who were quietly becoming drawn into the Golden State Killer vortex. One would become central to the story, and even give the serial murderer his now-famous moniker, the Golden State Killer.

Her name was Michelle McNamara, a writer from the Chicago suburbs who was born into an Irish Catholic family in 1970. Since childhood, McNamara had been fascinated by crime, sparked by the still unsolved murder of a young woman named Kathleen Lombardo just blocks from the future writer's childhood home.

McNamara worked in Northern Ireland for a year in 1992. That September, she was sexually assaulted by a man she worked for. She later said the incident helped drive her interest and ultimate investigation into the Golden State Killer.

After Ireland, she moved to Los Angeles, where she dreamed of becoming a writer for TV or the movies. Crime was never far behind.

She launched a website called TrueCrimeDiary. Around 2011 or 2012, she became fascinated by the twisted crimes of the monster variously known as the East Area Rapist, the Original Night Stalker and the Visalia Ransacker, among other epithets. Stories she wrote on the case for *Los Angeles* magazine in 2013 and 2014 renewed interest in the investigations.

And she made a powerful friend and ally in the Contra Costa County District Attorney's Office, investigator Paul Holes.

"Michelle came into my life because of this case. Initially, I treated her as just another writer that wanted to write an article, which, at the time, that's what she was doing," Holes recalled.

"She was writing an article for *Los Angeles* magazine. And I was very standoffish with her. But as her and I talked, we clicked.

And eventually, as we continued to communicate leading up to the release of this article."

In 2013, it was becoming increasingly rare for reporters and cops to trust one another. McNamara was different. And so was Paul Holes.

"I divulged aspects of my investigation that were sensitive. And when her article came out, I was so nervous that she would burn me. But I saw that she didn't in the article. And at that point, I recognized I could trust her," Holes told NPR.

"Eventually, she came up to Contra Costa County, and we spent a day where I'm driving her around to various crime scenes in my county as well as far up as Davis, California. And we're talking the entire time. She's recording the conversation. The conversation is about the cases, but it's also personal in terms of – you know, she's telling me about her upbringing, her marriage to Patton [Oswalt, the comedian], the lifestyle that she's living down there in the Los Angeles area married to a celebrity. And she's getting to know me. And we really bonded."

The mutual respect between cop and writer became so profound that Holes said they "became investigative partners". At the time, he was on the task force while she was busy writing a book about the case that would become a bestseller, *I'll Be Gone in the Dark: One Woman's Obsessive Search for the Golden State Killer*.

"She's the one that came up with the moniker Golden State Killer. I had always known this offender as East Area Rapist up until the time Michelle renamed him," Holes said. "And I argued with her about it, 'No, we don't need another name for this guy.' But turns out she was right to. The Golden State Killer is a much more descriptive moniker than East Area Rapist or Original Night Stalker."

Not content to record the investigation and Holes's and others' insights, McNamara was investigating the Golden State

Killer in her own right. Holes said that with his friend, writing often took a backseat to the investigation.

"And it's a huge case. There's a lot of pressure. When you start looking at the – you know, you have 15,000 pages of case file information," Holes said.

"Imagine how long it would take to read a novel that's 15,000 pages long. So it's a lot of data to go through, and it's the emotional roller coaster ride – Michelle, just like I experienced, thinking, 'Oh, I found a guy.' He looks good. And then, ultimately, the DNA shows he's not the guy. And that's an emotional crash. And so she's experiencing that. Plus, she has the pressure of writing the book."

I'll Be Gone in the Dark was about two-thirds finished when tragedy struck.

On the night of 21 April 2016, McNamara died suddenly in her sleep at her Los Angeles home. She was just 46 years old. An autopsy report obtained by the website Radar said her death was caused by the effects of numerous prescription drugs. The deadly cocktail included Adderall, fentanyl and Xanax. The website reported that some of the pharmaceuticals had not been prescribed to her.

In addition, cocaine and levamisole were also discovered. McNamara also had heart disease that had gone undiagnosed. Ultimately, the coroner ruled her death an accidental overdose.

In 2020, her husband, Patton Oswalt, and *I'll Be Gone in the Dark* director Liz Garbus revealed that McNamara had been suffering from opioid addiction.

McNamara's unexpected death hit Paul Holes hard. Not only had he lost a close friend and investigative partner, but there was also a treasure trove of new evidence to scour.

"My last communication with Michelle was – you know, she was driving up. She had a young daughter who was in the Girl Scouts, and she was taking her daughter to some sort of camp, I think just north of Santa Barbara," Holes recalled.

"And Michelle emails me just saying, 'Hey, passing through Santa Barbara where the Golden State Killer had attacked three times, had killed four people.' And she's passing the exits that he likely would have had to take in order to get out to commit these crimes. And she says, 'This is just such a surreal place to be with my daughter for Girl Scouts as I'm passing through where these horrific crimes occurred.' And then she just ended that email, you know, 'Talk soon.'"

McNamara's manuscript was finished by fellow true crime writers Paul Haynes and Billy Jensen and her widower, Patton Oswalt. *I'll Be Gone in the Dark* was released posthumously on 27 February 2018 and reached number 2 on *The New York Times* Bestseller list for non-fiction and number 1 on the combined print and e-book nonfiction.

McNamara died just days after her final conversation with Holes. Before that, she was scanning hundreds of documents and putting them in a file transfer service for the detective.

"I received an email from that file transfer service that there was something from Michelle waiting for me," Holes said. "I received that email after I found out she had died. And I went and downloaded that file. And it's – you know, in some ways, she was still helping me, so …"

McNamara's tome earned rave notices for its grit, candour and research. In 2018, HBO bought the rights to the book.

Yet, for all the Herculean efforts by McNamara and generations of detectives, the Golden State Killer remained at large. The rapes and murders, ice cold. The victims, shattered.

But partly due to McNamara's effort, the story of the Golden State Killer and his sick crimes was gaining traction. It also caught the attention of the Federal Bureau of Investigation – the famed FBI.

On 15 June 2016, the FBI released additional information related to the horrific crime spree, including new composite sketches and details of the crimes. The feds also offered a

$50,000 reward. In addition, the bold new initiative also included a national database to help support law enforcement's investigation of the crimes and to take tips and information.

"If he is still alive, the killer would now be approximately 60 to 75 years old. He is described as a white male, close to six feet tall, with blond or light brown hair and an athletic build," the FBI said in a news release. "He may have an interest or training in military or law enforcement techniques, and he was proficient with firearms.

"Detectives have DNA from multiple crime scenes that can positively link – or eliminate – suspects. This will allow investigators to easily rule out innocent parties with a simple, non-invasive DNA test."

It seemed as though homicide detectives had everything they needed, except the killer's real name.

Authorities also released a brief, disturbing recording of what they believed was the suspect's voice.

"People who know the subject may not believe him capable of such crimes," the FBI added. "He may not have exhibited violent tendencies or have a criminal history."

It had been 40 years since the mysterious killer struck, first with burglaries, ramping up to rape and finally, murder. He raped at least 45 women, killed at least 12 people and burglarized more than 120 homes. His victims were anywhere from 13 to 41 years old.

The FBI described him as "violent and elusive".

The agency pleaded with the public who lived in his numerous playgrounds up and down California to remember if they knew or remembered anyone who matched the suspect's physical description. The FBI noted that their suspect had a propensity to collect small items, particularly coins, ID cards and women's jewellery, from his crime scenes.

"It may push somebody over the edge who knows something," Sergeant Paul Belli, the Sacramento County Sheriff's Department detective assigned to the case, said at the time. "It could provide us with that one tip we need."

He added, "This serial offender was probably one of the most prolific, certainly in California and possibly within the United States."

In a bitterly ironic twist, the FBI made the announcement two days before the 40th anniversary of the culprit's first rape on 18 June 1976.

It wasn't quite the end of the road for the Golden State Killer, but the finish was in sight.

15

Science Catches Up

By the fall and early winter of 2017, the sands in the hourglass of Joseph James DeAngelo's evasion of justice were running out. The journey for cops, victims and their survivors had been very long indeed.

Every weapon that could be utilized was used. Sometimes it turns the tide; sometimes it doesn't. In the war against the Golden State Killer, the investigation started and then stopped again, countless times over four decades.

In 2001, cops believed they may have been getting close. DNA had definitively linked the East Area Rapist to the Original Night Stalker. The rapist and killer were the same man.

DNA is great, but if you still don't have a suspect and their genetic footprint is not in the Combined DNA Index System (CODIS), then you are most likely out of luck unless the perp gets pinched and is forced to submit a sample.

But in the background, the law enforcement equivalent of an atomic bomb was being developed. It would have profound consequences for a legion of old killers who thought they had got away with it. One of the first to be ensnared in the cops' new super weapon was a former Sacramento-area policeman named Joseph James DeAngelo.

The magic bullet, in layman's terms, was called genetic genealogy. And like a ghost from the past, it was reaching into the present day to bring justice to the dead and consequences to their killers. In some instances, the cold cases went back more than 60 years.

"This technique is really what genealogists were using to help adoptees find their biological parents," retired investigator Paul Holes said. "And it's a matter of taking your unknown DNA – our Golden State Killer DNA – searching the various genealogy DNA databases that we're permitted to search."

From this, investigators would obtain a list of relatives likely to share the suspect's DNA. Then they do "straight genealogy", using public records and old newspapers to build a family tree that would enable investigators to identify a common ancestor, somebody that the suspect – in this case, the Golden State Killer – would be a descendant of.

"And then building that family tree down into the current time and getting a list of names of people who all have a California connection, are the right age, and we just start investigating these individuals to try to determine, do they circumstantially add up to being somebody we need to get a direct DNA sample from to compare to the DNA that we have from the crime scenes of the Golden State Killer?"

Since 2017, the miracle tech has solved an infinite number of mysteries. From unsolved homicides to unidentified bodies to missing persons, it has made a massive difference to investigators, the survivors, and maybe even the dead.

"It is a total game changer," according to Detective Sergeant Steve Smith, the Toronto Police Service cold case unit commander. "We can solve almost anything now as long as we have DNA."

Smith's team have cleared a slew of cases that have vexed detectives for decades, and scores more are on deck for clearance.

Toronto cops have not been alone in employing the method to solve cases. Philadelphia Police solved one of the most infamous unsolved cases in American history when they identified the tragic "Boy in the Box" in 2022. He became known as America's Unknown Child.

On 25 February 1957, at around 10:40 a.m., the body of the little boy – believed to be between the ages of four and six – was found inside a cardboard JCPenney bassinet box in a wooded area of Philadelphia's Fox Chase neighbourhood.

The boy was naked and had been severely beaten. His body was covered in bruises, and he had suffered severe head trauma. He was also severely malnourished, weighing just 30 pounds (14 kg). The coroner said he died from blunt force trauma to the head.

Despite relentless flyer campaigns and press coverage, no one ever came forward to identify the little murder victim who became known as the Boy in the Box.

"There is a profound sadness," Philly's Police Commissioner Danielle Outlaw told reporters in 2022. "His entire identity was taken away. No one should have to wait this long for the story of their life to be told."

The boy's final resting spot was in plot 191 in one of the city's potter's fields. Homicide detectives served as his pallbearers and paid for a headstone. These tireless cops became the tragic little boy's guardians, the parents he never had in life. And they desperately wanted to catch his killers.

But the case went cold fast, despite a tidal wave of national media coverage. Cops never made much headway on the boy's identity or who killed him, despite heroic efforts over the decades. As long as they couldn't identify this tragic child, solving his murder would be just out of reach.

In 1998, his body was exhumed to extract DNA. There wasn't enough, and he was reinterred, this time at Ivy Hill

Cemetery – again, under the loving eyes of the Philadelphia Police Department's homicide unit.

With forensic science changing every day, the still-unidentified boy's remains were exhumed again in 2019. This time, genealogists used the boy's DNA to research possible relatives and eventually established the identity of his birth parents.

On 8 December 2022, police held a press conference to announce that after 65 years, 9 months and 13 days, they had identified the little boy as Joseph Augustus Zarelli. He had been born on 13 January 1953 and was just four years old when he was murdered.

"It's going to be an uphill battle for us to definitively determine who caused this child's death," emotional Philadelphia Homicide Captain Jason Smith said in 2022.

"If this technology had been available to us 20 years ago, it might be a completely different story, because once you identify who the child is, you start interviewing family members. Well, at this point in time, a lot of the family members who would have been old enough to have a memory of any incident that might have occurred are normally long gone."

Little Joseph was from West Philadelphia, and he had half-siblings. A Social Security number was never issued for Joseph, Smith added.

"This time, detectives were able to locate relatives on the maternal side and identify his birth mother," Smith said, explaining that the paternal part of the equation followed.

Using the same technique that would eventually nab the Golden State Killer, police identified Joseph by using genetic testing and investigative genetic genealogy. According to cops, genealogists had finally uncovered Joseph's name in October 2021. A cousin had uploaded their DNA to a public database.

Detectives then encouraged the cousin's mother (a first cousin of the boy) to submit her DNA to GEDmatch. That allowed police to identify the Boy in the Box's parents. They then applied for a court order to get the child's birth certificate, revealing the long-hidden names of his parents, which were later verified via DNA.

"We have our suspicions as to who may be responsible, but it would be irresponsible of me to share these suspicions," Smith said, adding his investigators were "hopeful" someone would remember Joseph.

"I don't know what the neighbours knew or didn't know. The child did live past the age of four years old, so there would have been somebody out there that would have seen this child, perhaps another family member that hasn't stepped forward, possibly a neighbour that remembers seeing that child, and remembers whatever was occurring at that particular household."

Now, the questions for homicide detectives were who killed the boy, what were the circumstances leading to his horrific death, and why was he killed?

The man named by *The Philadelphia Inquirer* as his biological father, Augustus John "Gus" Zarelli, reportedly had no idea that his then-girlfriend Mary Elizabeth (née Abel) Plunkett, known as "Betsy", was even pregnant.

After the Golden State Killer, the Boy in the Box was the jewel in the crown of genetic genealogy. But there have been hundreds of other historic homicides and unidentified remains investigations that have now been cleared in the past decade.

The Toronto Police cold case unit has solved more than 58 homicides, unidentified remains, and sexual assaults in three years using genetic genealogy. The unit's boss, Detective Sergeant Steve Smith is one of the law enforcement world's chief proponents of the groundbreaking tech. He spoke directly to the author on several occasions during research for this book, and explained how it works.

"The DNA that we use for court purposes is STR data, Short Tandem Repeat. So that's basically your 22 genetic markers. Everybody's genetically different. It's great for one-to-one matching because it can show without a shred of a doubt that you are the person who left the DNA at the crime scene," the veteran detective said.

"But what it isn't good at is finding anything in between. So if you have an unheld DNA profile at the scene and the person isn't on either the National DNA Data Bank or CODIS, well, now all you've got is, you know that some male in the world left his DNA there. How do you find that male?"

He added, "It's a needle in a haystack."

Investigative genetic genealogy (IGG) is if you use a special processor, then change the DNA from STR data to what's called an SNP (single nucleotide polymorphism), and those are the genes between family trees.

"And if you do it well, if you sequence it well, it can be 500,000 to a million SNPs, so you can get everything that tells you how related you are to everybody else," Smith said.

"So instead of finding the differences, you find similarities. Once you get that SNP, if it's definitive enough, you upload it to the database, maybe GEDmatch or Family Tree DNA, and then you get matches of who in the world has uploaded their DNA to those databases, and then if it agrees, police involvement."

It was genetic genealogy that finally solved one of Toronto's most notorious unsolved murders, which at one point sent an innocent man to prison.

Christine Jessop was nine years old when she vanished on 3 October 1984 on her way to her Queensville home in the suburbs of Toronto after school. Christine's body was discovered in a wooded area about 25 miles (40 km) away. She had been raped and strangled to death.

Cops zeroed in on an oddball neighbour named Guy Paul Morin, who was subsequently arrested and wrongfully convicted of her death. He was later cleared in 1995.

Many aspects of the original investigation were botched and impeded by the investigative limitations of the time.

Thirty-six years later, using genetic genealogy via the famed Othram Laboratories in Texas, Toronto Police announced that they had identified Christine's killer. He was a cable installer named Calvin Hoover, who was a family friend of the Jessops and whose children had been playmates of the dead girl.

"With Jessop, we started with two matches, but because of the automatic knockout after the Golden State Killer stuff."

Before the Golden State Killer, the databases were wide-open, but privacy concerns triggered a rethink on the part of labs.

"There was a case in Utah where an old lady was a pianist in a church, and she got beaten up, but lived," Smith recalled, adding cops got the perpetrator.

"But the people at GEDmatch said the police breached their terms of service because they were only supposed to use it for sexual assaults, homicides and UHRs (Unidentified Human Remains)."

Afterwards, GEDmatch went from an automatic opt-in to an automatic opt-out. People using genetic genealogy, if they wanted their DNA accessible to cops, had to opt back in.

"So when we uploaded [DNA from the Jessop case], we had two matches. One on the maternal side, one on the paternal side. We had 32,000 people in our tree to start," Smith said. "Having one match from each side gave us a huge heads-up."

Both Hoover's maternal and paternal sides had emigrated to Belleville, a small city two hours east of Toronto. Cops were now basically mapping out all of Belleville.

"That's why we had, say, 32,000 people in our tree. And from there, we started to contact people who had trees up on paper and asked them if they could put it over to GEDmatch, who were able to cut out huge portions of the tree," Smith said.

"That took us down to about 5,000 people. So we got down to about 5,000 people, and then we went back and got the $700 US to upload the family tree's DNA. When we did that, we got over 100 matches on the family tree DNA, so at that point we were right into two first cousins. It was just which one was it going to be?"

It was Calvin Hoover.

Smith added, "And that's how it works."

Hoover would never have to answer for the heinous crime. He killed himself in 2015, five years before he was identified as the child killer. Hoover was one of the few people who knew that the Jessops would be away on the day of the murder and Christine wasn't going with them.

No one had ever suspected Hoover. His alibi had checked out, and his wife later told reporters she had "absolutely no idea" of the evil that lurked within. She now believes the murder of Christine weighed heavily on her late husband and sent him into a booze-fuelled "downward spiral".

The book isn't quite closed on Calvin Hoover. He travelled extensively for his job in Canada, as well as several cities in the United States. Detectives are still trying to determine whether the killer might be connected to any other unsolved murders.

Christine's father, Ken Jessop, always believed Hoover was responsible for the disappearance and suspected murder of another Toronto girl named Nicole Morin. Nicole, eight, was meeting a pal at her apartment pool and vanished into thin air. Her disappearance on 30 July 1985 came less than a year after Christine was murdered.

Detective Sergeant Steve Smith said investigators have diligently explored this theory, but they've yet to find any evidence linking the cable installer to Nicole's building at the time.

"Oh, we looked at him for everything. We mapped out everywhere. He travelled a lot, extensively," Smith explained. "He loved gambling, so he went to Vegas and those places a lot, but he also travelled for work throughout the US. So we reached out to a ton of different police services there to see if anything may match, but nothing came out of it."

As far as cops know, the sickening depravity Calvin Hoover unleashed that dark day in 1983 was a one-off.

"Well, as far as we know, but with that sort of crime, it's a bit of if it looks like a duck, walks like a duck ... Yeah, I'm sure there are other things, but we just haven't been able to put it together."

In the intervening years since the capture or identification of the Golden State Killer, Calvin Hoover, and hundreds of other aged killers, the rules surrounding genetic genealogy have changed, so the cops have had to alter how they use the cold case atomic bomb.

"When the Golden State Killer came through, they had access to the whole [genetic] database," Smith said, adding that genetic databases are becoming more diverse.

"In the beginning, if your offender had any sort of Northern European in them, you're almost guaranteed to find them because a large portion of the database, especially back then, was Northern European-based. If you had a white Northern European person, it was very easy to find matches. And then from there, you start building family trees, you build back in time to find the most recent common ancestors. Once you find the most recent common ancestors, you find out how the families interacted with each other, and it leads you back down towards your offender's unknown DNA. And you can narrow it down to a family to say, 'This is a family that produced the offenders.'"

Two women were raped and murdered in Toronto just months apart in 1983. DNA would later finger the same perpetrator in both investigations.

"The genetic genealogy led to a family who lived around 700 miles (1125 km) north of Toronto. There were five brothers, and one of them was the killer," Smith said. "And that's just the point of eliminating, collecting the DNA to eliminate each one."

The veteran homicide detective admits that the process seems simple, but it still requires the old police standby of shoe leather, literal or figurative.

"It could still take years on end to try and figure out who your actual offender is," he said.

"But genetic genealogy, that's been a massive game changer. A lot of the cases we've solved sat unsolved for decades, and now … they're going boom, boom, boom, boom. You might have had the unknown DNA profile, but you had no idea who it was. Now you're able to actually narrow it down and figure out who it actually is. So it's a huge difference.

"Criminals should be very scared. I would have loved to have done the door knock and seen Calvin Hoover's face when he saw us, then watch him squirm in court."

On a daily basis, cold case detectives across North America are solving cases that were once considered unsolvable. Nearly impossible investigations have been given new life and new hope to the families of the dead and missing.

But the common perception has been that the miracle of genetic genealogy being used by the police started with Joseph James DeAngelo Jr. Its antecedents can be traced to the 1981 disappearances of a young New Hampshire mom and her baby daughter.

Contra Costa County investigator Paul Holes learned about genetic genealogy from another harrowing California investigation while researching the perpetrator's background.

"I found that he had been arrested for child abandonment in 1986," Holes said. "The child that he abandoned was this little girl named Lisa Jenson. We started looking into this for the more recent homicide case that occurred in 2002, and he was claiming Lisa was his biological daughter, and DNA quickly showed that [she] wasn't."

The lead detective on the case became convinced that Lisa had probably been abducted from somewhere in the United States and was a missing girl somewhere else. Investigators had spent 15 years trying to discover Lisa's real identity using traditional DNA testing and conventional law enforcement techniques, but they could never seal the deal.

There were a staggering number of red herrings and twists in the probe, with tentacles spreading across the US, countless dead ends, false names and a litany of other roadblocks. The deep dive stemmed from a murder in Contra Costa County.

Former homicide detective Roxane Gruenheid found the body of chemist Eunsoon Jun in 2003 and put her killer behind bars. But she was uneasy about the killer and his mysterious past that continued to nag at her. Gruenheid didn't believe the conviction and imprisonment was the last she would hear of the murderer who gave the name "Curtis Kimball".

Kimball had pleaded guilty to killing the 44-year-old Jun, and the pair had been dating before she disappeared. It was Gruenheid who found Jun's dismembered body in her Richmond, California, home in the Bay Area. The killer's story kept changing after he originally pleaded no contest to the second-degree murder charge.

Soon, Curtis Kimball told detectives that his name was Larry Vanner. He had also used the name Gordon Jenson.

Something about Kimball, or whoever he really was, kept gnawing at her. He was a proven liar and had served time for child abandonment for deserting a little girl he called his 5-year-old daughter, Lisa, 15 years earlier.

"I was really centred on the little girl, on Lisa," Gruenheid told ABC News. "Like, was this really his daughter? … If it's not his daughter, where did he get her? Who did he get her from?"

She said of his guilty plea: "I think … he believed if he pled guilty … I would stop investigating that aspect of his past."

It would take years to discover the full scope of Kimball's crime and determine he was, in fact, a cross-country serial killer who preyed on women and children and used multiple aliases. The killer's real name was Terry Peder Rasmussen, who, like DeAngelo, had served in the US Navy during the Vietnam War.

Investigators gave Rasmussen his moniker: "The Chameleon".

Oddly, the Rasmussen investigation never received much national attention despite its gruesome and intriguing nature. While the case didn't get barrels of ink, it changed the nature of forensic investigations forever with the use of genetic genealogy.

"In February 2017, I got pulled into a conference call with the lead investigator from that case, as well as a San Bernardino detective, Peter Headly. And Headly said that they had identified Lisa, and it turned out her name was Dawn Beaudin, and she was a missing girl out of New Hampshire," Holes recalled.

"I said, 'How did you do that?' And he said, 'I used a genetic genealogist through DNAAdoption.com. Her name was Barbara Rae-Venter.'"

Holes added, "So when I left from that meeting, from that case, I called up Barbara, and was like, 'I've got this other case. Could you help me with this?'"

16

Searching for Rot in the Family Tree

Genealogist Barbara Rae-Venter spent her working career as a patent attorney. Not exactly the gruesome territory of serial killers.

When she retired after a successful career, on her wish list was embarking on a journey of discovery and digging into her family history. In addition, she also hoped to play some tennis and do some travelling.

"And, as I started doing my family history research, I started getting matches with people who were adopted," she told ISHI News in 2019. "And, I really didn't know how to help them find their birth relatives. So, I took an online class through a group called DNAAdoption, and what they do is they teach you how to do genetic genealogy."

She added, "At one point, there was a detective in San Bernardino who contacted us and wanted some help on a case. That was the Lisa Jenson case, which got me started on doing all this."

Contra Costa County cold case investigator Paul Holes had a colleague who had worked with Rae-Venter, and it got him thinking about his long elusive nemesis, the Golden State Killer. He was familiar with the Jenson case.

Holes began wondering whether genetic genealogy might help finally close the Golden State Killer case. With the clock ticking on his law enforcement career, he asked himself whether this could be his final gambit in identifying and, if he was alive, capturing the killer.

"At a certain point, in 2017, that's when I ran across Barbara, and what she had done in that Lisa Jenson case, because I had a connection to that case. And I was like, how did that happen? So, I had reached out to Barbara, saying, 'I need help on this,'" Holes said.

"I didn't even tell her what case it was. I think I said something like, 'It's a cold case, but it would be a feather in your cap, because it's such a big case.' And she's like, 'Sure, send me what you've got.' And then I didn't hear from her. And then she pops up in, what, six months later, and she said, 'Hey, do you still need some help?' And I was like, 'Yes! Please!'"

First, as the Visalia Ransacker, then as the East Area Rapist, and then as the Original Night Stalker, Holes's quarry had eluded numerous law enforcement agencies for 42 years. He was clever, and he was unbelievably lucky. And by this point in 2017, other than a few taunting phone calls, the Golden State Killer had been dormant for 31 or 32 years.

Police had the serial killer's DNA for years and even determined that the same perpetrator was responsible for the crimes that stretched from Sacramento to Orange County. If the suspect's DNA had been in the system, they would have had him by now, but it was not.

In almost all cold case murders, the case is typically solved by either a change in circumstances or relationships or … new technology. For the Golden State Killer, it would be the latter.

Once Holes connected with Barbara Rae-Venter, the investigation unfolded rapidly.

"It took us about, what, four-and-a-half months. Once we got the initial DNA results, four-and-a-half months to the time that DeAngelo was taken into custody," Holes said.

The pair were mostly working remotely using email and the phone. There were also two law enforcement personnel working on the murders in Southern California and two more in Sacramento.

And then, they began the painstaking work of building family trees.

"We created a centralized account in order to be able to do all of the genealogy work, and so we are just remotely, for the most part, doing this. And Barbara would take a look at the trees that we were building and tell us what we were doing wrong and correct us," Holes said.

"And then that's really how we were interacting. Now, of course, I'm interfacing with the law enforcement guys on the team every now and then. So, I'm going up to Sacramento, or I'm meeting with the FBI."

Throughout the genetic genealogy aspect of the investigation, Holes and Rae-Venter met just once, and that was at a watering hole near San Diego.

Holes said that cops followed Rae-Venter's lead and her innovative technique.

"That technique has touched off such a revolution within law enforcement, and so many other cases have been solved using it," he said.

The world was a very different place in 2017 from when Joseph James DeAngelo Jr embarked on his sadistic campaign of sexual violence. Now, the walls were closing in, and it's unlikely he was even aware of it.

He rode his bike, tended to his lawn, looked after his granddaughter and was looking forward to retirement after 27 years working as a mechanic for a supermarket chain. And deep in the darkest recesses of his soul, DeAngelo probably believed that he had gotten away with murder.

Perhaps not the perfect crimes, but fairly close. He had no inkling the finish line was near.

And every two weeks, like clockwork, DeAngelo would drive the 12 miles (19 km) from his home in suburban Citrus Heights to the all-nude Gold Club Centerfolds in Rancho Cordova. At the club, the young dancers described him as a "creepy old racist".

Unlikeable, sure, but no one at the club would have pegged him for a serial killer and sadist – one of the most notorious monsters in California history.

Yet one dancer told the *Daily Mail* in 2018 that she witnessed DeAngelo become unhinged when a fellow stripper suggested he take a DNA test to prove he was 100 per cent white himself. The man who sat at a table in the middle of the club close to the stage then became "sweaty and stuttery", the dancer told the tabloid.

"All of a sudden, he got stressed out for no real reason," the 21-year-old stripper said. "Now I think I know why."

On the evening of his racist explosion, DeAngelo called the non-white guests in the room "nasty and dirty".

"I've only been working here since January. I work three or four nights a week, and I have seen him here at least four times, so, yeah, he's a regular," the stripper said. "I never saw him spend a dime; he never asked for lap dances."

She added, "He sat back from the stage so he wasn't expected to tip the girls as they danced. He would just pay his entrance money, come in and stare at the girls. He would be there at about five or six o'clock and maybe stay for a couple of hours."

The stripper said that initially, she thought the grumpy old man was funny and charming. He told her his name was Joe and that he was a retired cop. But he was mercurial, and not every dancer got the same treatment.

DeAngelo boasted to his favoured dancers that he had guns and could protect them. He had a "quirky grandfatherly feeling". And that's the way it was until the night of his racist outburst.

"Out of the blue, he suddenly told me his girlfriend had sex with her sister," the dancer told the British newspaper. "Then he said: 'It's an Indian thing.'

"I said: 'What do you mean, like Indian from India or Native American?' and he said, 'Native American.' Then he told me how he hated the fact that she was Native American and suddenly launched into a really horrible racist rant, pointing to everyone in the club who wasn't white and calling them nasty and dirty.

"I told him he should be careful, perhaps he should take one of those DNA tests you see on TV to see if he's all white – I don't know why I thought of it, I think I'd just seen an advertisement for one of them.

"He got all strange and wiped his hand over his face and said: 'They'll never get my DNA.' But he said his sister had taken one of those tests. He got all sweaty and stuttery. Now it makes sense."

Still, while DeAngelo was standoffish, he generally behaved and didn't attempt to grope any of the girls.

And the young blonde dancer didn't believe there was a girlfriend. She guessed the girlfriend was a prostitute or someone he paid for sex.

After his racist explosion, the dancer tried to avoid the "quirky" customer. He still tried to talk to her, she said.

Another dancer said DeAngelo was "grumpy and standoffish" and had a reputation as a miser, and that got around the club, so most of the dancers avoided the freeloader.

The young women who were taking off their clothes for cold, hard cash had no idea that if DeAngelo gave them the creeps, there was a good reason for it.

Generations were haunted by his frightening rape and murder spree. Adding to the mystery and fears was the reality that he remained unencumbered by prison bars or the hot seat of the execution chamber.

Cold case investigator Paul Holes was desperate to solve the Golden State Killer case before the sun set on his wildly successful career of bringing monsters to justice.

"I would like to think that we would have been able to solve this case and prevent further victimization," Holes said. "DNA does do this. There's other tools, there's other investigative aspects that get the bad guys off the street and prevent them from re-offending, but when you take a look at these kinds of crimes, like the Golden State Killer cases, and the horrific experiences that both people that are still alive today that were victimized and lived with that trauma or the people that lost their lives, and the family members and all the pain that they still experience to this day, if this tool had been available back then, my hope would be that we would have found DeAngelo and at least saved some of those lives."

One of the problems Holes faced as the buzzer approached on his career was a diminishing supply of the killer's DNA. He had samples from three Contra Costa cases, but as technology evolved, more and more of the samples were put through the various processes.

"But over time, as different technologies came on board, I'm dipping and consuming more and more of that DNA," Holes said.

"Then, we start looking at well, there's this genealogy side with Y-STRs, so I end up consuming everything else I had thinking, 'CODIS isn't doing it for me, so maybe genealogy with Y-STRs will do it.' I didn't know anything about the SNP testing at all. I spent six years pursuing the Y-STR leads, and then I find out about SNPs.

"I have no more DNA left. So the challenge at this point was me reaching out to the Southern California agencies with homicides and asking them, 'Do you have any DNA left in your cases?' And some of them did not, or they never had enough, or the type of DNA, because it was too mixed with the victim's DNA, and it just didn't work."

But Holes struck pay dirt with Ventura County. Specifically, DNA collected from sexual assault kits in the Lyman and Charlene Smith double homicide. The pathologist at the time provided cops one sample, and another went to the county coroner's office.

His colleagues in Ventura had done the same thing: dipping into the DNA as technology changed.

"Then myself and [FBI Agent] Steve Kramer went and briefed Ventura about this new tool that Barbara was championing, and we're saying, 'Do you still have any DNA left?'," Holes said.

"That investigator from Ventura starts digging, and he discovers that untouched sexual assault kit, and it turned out to have a gold mine of Golden State Killer DNA in it."

Law enforcement began zeroing in on DeAngelo in December 2017. Holes and the FBI and Kramer uploaded the killer's DNA profile using a Ventura County rape kit to GEDmatch. The website identified between 10 and 20 people who had the same great-great-great-grandparents as the suspect.

Through the winter and spring of 2018, using genetic genealogy, investigators did countless comparisons and built an endless number of family trees.

Using genetic genealogy on GEDmatch, investigators finally identified relatives of DeAngelo. Family members were directly related to the suspected killer's great-great-great-great-grandfather, who lived in the 1800s.

Police constructed 25 different family trees. To underscore the digital shoe leather required to close the case, the family tree that detectives eventually linked to Joseph James DeAngelo Jr contained around 1,000 individuals.

In many ways, DNA and genetic genealogy are not magic bullets, but what they provide are shortcuts. A pool of 1,000 potential suspects is easier to deal with than a pool of 100,000.

Police then began looking at other clues such as age, sex and where the people lived to rule out suspects. They were ruled out, painstakingly, one by one, until just one name remained on the list.

Joseph James DeAngelo.

***

It later emerged that law enforcement could have had their man in 1996 in a comical episode that may have been a once-in-a-lifetime opportunity to crack the puzzle of the Golden State Killer.

Authorities would say that DeAngelo was never on their radar. This 1996 episode proves otherwise.

According to *The Sacramento Bee*, DeAngelo was arrested in Placer County for an alleged "gas and dash" (filling a car with petrol and leaving without paying). DeAngelo was innocent, and details of the incident were gleaned from a $1 million civil suit he filed against the owner of the gas station.

According to reports, on 28 July 1995, DeAngelo was filling his tank and attempting to pre-pay at the pump. Unfortunately for DeAngelo, the pump malfunctioned before he had filled his tank with the pre-set amount. He went inside and asked the attendant for a refund.

"When he attempted to inform the clerk that the pump was not working and asked for his change for the gas not pumped, the clerk became uncooperative, apparently not able to speak English well enough to understand plaintiff," a 20 February 1998 settlement conference statement in the court file states.

"Plaintiff left the premises peacefully, and subsequently, the clerk called police and reported plaintiff as an attempted robber. Some eight months later plaintiff was arrested by police in a sting operation where letters were sent informing plaintiff and others that they had [won] a prize. Plaintiff was required to bail and hire an attorney. Eventually, the case was dismissed and the court entered an order finding plaintiff factually innocent and sealed the records."

His only other brush with the law had been the 1979 shoplifting incident that had cost him his job with the Auburn Police Department.

It was years before criminals had to submit to mandatory DNA testing. In addition, there was nothing out of the ordinary about the arrest. No red flags or banners were screaming, "This man is a serial killer."

"We had no way of knowing at the time who we actually had in our jail because the evidence wasn't there, the technology wasn't there," Sacramento Sheriff's Sergeant Shaun Hampton said. "I don't think there's any way we could have known; there was no way for us to identify this person by him simply being in our jail for a few hours."

His lawyer in the gas station lawsuit remembered "Joe" as a "nice guy" who was "very upset about this gas station business".

"What they did was, they contacted several people – I don't know how he got on the list – and told them they had won free Super Bowl tickets and got them down there in this auditorium," lawyer William Wright told the *Bee*. "And the cops busted all of them because they had either warrants or were wanted."

Time and technology (or lack thereof) continued to work in the former cop's favour.

Several years following the gas pump problem, the Sacramento Sheriff's Department began collecting DNA from new felony arrests. California-wide collection didn't start until 2004 with Proposition 69, ironically, an initiative bankrolled by Bruce Harrington, whose brother and sister-in-law, Keith and Patrice Harrington, were murdered by the Golden State Killer in August 1980.

DeAngelo's case was eventually settled out of court and dismissed.

His lawyer didn't recognize his former client until his face was plastered all over the TV and newspapers.

"I'd seen the guy on TV, but I never made the connection," Wright said. "He was very pleasant when he was talking to me."

But that was 1996. Now, in 2018, there would be no bye, no free pass, no absurd luck.

The team were positive that the gruff elderly man was the killer. But they had to be certain. After all, the genetic genealogy appeared to be the cops' last chance saloon until the next scientific advance, which could be years in the future.

On 18 April 2018, a DNA sample was surreptitiously collected from the door handle of DeAngelo's car. Later, another sample was collected from a discarded tissue found in DeAngelo's kerbside garbage can.

Both samples were then matched to those left behind by the Golden State Killer.

On 19 April 2018, the results came back: James Joseph DeAngelo Jr was the Golden State Killer. He was put under round-the-clock surveillance.

Now, there was "overwhelming evidence" that after more than four decades, the long elusive rapist and murderer had been positively identified. The discarded tissue was the cherry on top, leaving absolutely no doubts.

"The second sample was astronomical evidence that it was him," District Attorney Anne Marie Schubert told *The Sacramento Bee*.

This breakthrough extended beyond the victims and their survivors. A man who was 12 years old during the East Area Rapist's nights of terror said he had a sliding glass door on his bedroom. At night, he'd stick a dowel in it and take his BB gun to bed with him.

"And I hear that over and over again," Holes said. "People that lived in Sacramento at the time that the East Area Rapist was attacking, who was the same person as the Golden State Killer. Or, even in Davis, where there's only three attacks. But because of the type of attack and who he's attacking. He's attacking just the everyday people in their own homes. Anybody could have become his victims. So, it caused fear in the community, because everybody is recognizing, 'I could be a victim of this guy.'"

The Golden State Killer earned one more victory, albeit a pyrrhic one, over his long-time nemesis Paul Holes. The veteran investigator and cold case trailblazer had hung up his gun and badge, but cops on the ground kept him apprised of the situation on an hour-by-hour basis.

"I had retired. In fact, when he was under surveillance, I was out in Colorado with my wife, shopping for a house," Holes explained.

"And then I'm getting updates about the surveillance. And then, eventually, I get an update about an initial DNA sample, which was a mixed sample from his car door handle when he went to a Hobby Lobby."

Holes knew DeAngelo was the ghost he had, at times, fruitlessly been chasing for decades.

"But at that moment, it was like, I know that's the Golden State Killer. And so when I got back to California, I end up going up and being embedded within Sacramento homicide," Holes said.

"And myself and a Sacramento homicide sergeant, Ken Clark, we lock ourselves in Ken's office and write the arrest warrant. And then I assist on the search warrant – just waiting for that second sample […] the piece of tissue, to get results back.

"And once that came back, then Ken was able to get the judge to sign it. And DeAngelo was arrested."

17

Arrest and Charges

On Tuesday, 24 April 2018, around 5:30 p.m. Pacific time, the long, bleak drama of the Golden State Killer reached its climax. The final act was at hand.

Joseph James DeAngelo Jr was arrested at his home on Canyon Oak Drive in Citrus Heights by heavily armed police officers of the Sacramento Sheriff's Department. The story was a blockbuster on the national news cycle, and media worldwide reported on the dramatic arrest.

DeAngelo's arrest came after years of dogged investigation, persistence, and bad luck. He had instilled fear in some of the state's most benign precincts.

Now, the world finally got a good look at the Golden State Killer and his precursors, the Visalia Ransacker, the East Area Rapist and the Original Night Stalker. He was a balding, 72-year-old man who shuffled and carried a perpetually sour look on his face.

"In a perfectly executed arrest, my detectives arrested James Joseph DeAngelo, 72 years old, living in Citrus Heights," Sacramento County Sheriff Scott Jones stated.

For generations of detectives who had pursued the killer, there was joy and a sigh of relief. But there were also a lot of what-ifs, doubts and second-guessing.

And now, it was time to interrogate this violent enigma. Would he spill his guts or would he be tight-lipped? How detectives handled this delicate part of the probe would be crucial. Holes would be paired with Sacramento homicide detective Ken Clark.

"Ken and I had talked about a strategy in that Ken was going to go in initially, talk to him about the Sacramento cases," Paul Holes later told NPR. "And then Ken and I were going to interview DeAngelo regarding the other Northern California cases that I had a high level of familiarity with before allowing the Southern California homicide investigators to go in."

However, the wild card was going to be DeAngelo.

"But once Ken goes in for his initial interview on the Sacramento cases, it was obvious that DeAngelo wasn't going to talk. He literally sat in the interview room and stared at the other wall, not even paying attention to Ken, not responding to his questions," Holes recalled.

"And then, eventually, as that progressed, we recognized that talking to him about other sexual assaults in Northern California was not going to be a good experience for us. And we needed to let Southern California homicide investigators at least have a crack at him before he decided to invoke his rights for an attorney."

In many ways, police always had the answers, but they were in pieces, sometimes disparate bits of information that might have tied the case together sooner had they not been scattered like sawdust up and down California. If DNA beats shoe leather, then so be it.

In many ways, Joseph James DeAngelo Jr was exactly what Holes had envisioned for years. But in others, he was not.

"As I investigated the case, I really came to the conclusion that our offender is Sacramento-based, probably still living in the Sacramento area, which DeAngelo was. And I also concluded that I am dealing with a sophisticated and intelligent offender," Holes said.

"Turns out the offender, the Golden State Killer, was a former cop. He understood law enforcement tactics. He had been trained as an investigator for burglaries. So he had skill sets that were up and beyond the average person in order to be able to develop tactics and get away with these crimes."

Retired Contra Costa County Sheriff's Office lieutenant Larry Crompton was one of these cops. He was intimately involved in the investigation during the height of the crimes and wrote a book about the case in 2010, *Sudden Terror*, that later inspired Michelle McNamara.

"For many, many years, I would wake up at 3 o'clock in the morning and say, 'What did I do wrong? What did I miss?'" Crompton told KATU-TV. "It drove me nuts."

Crompton began hunting the prowler in 1978, before he became the Golden State Killer. Like a lot of investigators who worked the case, he was certain he was hunting an arch-criminal responsible for a multitude of vile crimes. In the 1970s, there was no DNA technology to point the finger.

And in the dying days of disco, the monster Crompton was hunting was the East Area Rapist.

"We knew that one person was doing the rapes and it was because of the way that the rapes were being done," Crompton said, adding that news of the arrest "sent chills up my back".

"The East Area Rapist had hit Sacramento and Modesto, Stockton and areas like that, 37 rapes. And we knew nothing about it. And even though Sacramento was only miles from us but in those days if you didn't live in that city or get that newspaper, you didn't know about those."

Like other detectives who worked on the case, Crompton became obsessed and helped to link the dots between the rapes and break-ins in Northern California and the slew of homicides further south. He aided cops in both Santa Barbara and Orange County.

For years, he said, investigators shared information about the far-flung crimes.

"He always wore a mask. He always wore gloves. He would talk to them with clenched teeth and whisper," Crompton said.

"And he would come back and put dishes on the man's back, and he would tell 'em, 'If I hear these rattle, I'll kill your wife. I'll kill you.' And if there was a child in the house, 'I'll cut the child's ears off and bring 'em to you.' The sex was not his priority. The terror that he put into them was his priority."

Crompton came to believe that one of the Golden State Killer's assets, keeping him unencumbered by the law, was his past as a police officer. He knew how law enforcement operated.

"For him to be in law enforcement while he was doing this just drives us nuts," he said. "'Cause that's not what we're there for. We're there to stop people like him."

DeAngelo was never on their radar. Crompton later echoed many other cops of the time, lamenting the lack of communication and cooperation – two unfortunate pitfalls that allowed the Golden State Killer to continue his murderous odyssey.

"Back then, agencies did not cooperate together," he said. "If they get an opportunity to talk to him and find out who he is, why he acted like that, how he did it, then I think it's gonna help law enforcement in the future … He was nowhere close to the most active but he was the most violent that they have ever had."

Following DeAngelo's arrest, Sacramento County District Attorney Anne Marie Schubert and Major Crimes Bureau

Assistant Chief Deputy DA Rod Norgaard filed felony complaints against DeAngelo for the murders of Brian and Katie Maggiore.

The double killing on 2 February 1978 carried the special circumstance of "multiple murders". That ticked the box for a date with the executioner.

In Ventura County, District Attorney Gregory Totten and Senior Deputy District Attorney Richard Simon allege that on or about 13 March 1980 through 1 March 1980, DeAngelo murdered Lyman and Charlene Smith. In Ventura, the authorities tagged on three special circumstances: multiple murders, murder during the commission of rape, and murder during the commission of burglary.

Again, another ticket to death row at San Quentin.

Authorities held a press conference on 25 April 2018, and in a bitter twist for DeAngelo, it was also National DNA Day.

"In the last six days, and I emphasize the last six days, that passion, that persistence, and the knowledge finally came to an answer in this building behind us here, our crime lab," Schubert told reporters.

DeAngelo was now behind bars at the Sacramento County jail.

Reporters were told that the long probe into the Golden State Killer was still an active investigation. Schubert added that it was not a tipster that led them to DeAngelo, but that "he was identified through DNA technology".

"We knew we could and should solve it using the most innovative DNA technology available at this time," Schubert said, adding the key was "crime lab employees, DNA analysts who worked tirelessly in the last few days to provide that answer".

Sheriff Scott Jones said DeAngelo had been under surveillance for a while.

"We were able to get some discarded DNA, and we were able to confirm what we thought we already knew. That we had our man," Jones said.

Orange County District Attorney Tony Rackauckas added: "Joseph James DeAngelo has been called a lot of things by law enforcement: he's been called the East Side Rapist, the Visalia Ransacker, the Original Night Stalker, and the Golden State Killer. Today, it's our pleasure to call him defendant."

Also speaking at the press conference was Bruce Harrington, whose younger brother Keith and his sister-in-law Patrice were murdered by the suspect. Harrington spent two decades and more than $2 million of his own money to reform DNA laws that would help resolve cases like the Golden State Killer.

"It's time for all victims to grieve and to take measure one last time," Harrington said. "To bring closure to the anguish that we've all suffered for the last 40-some-odd years. It is time for the victims to begin to heal. So long overdue."

He added, "To the entire reservoir of victims out there, my sadness is with you. For the 51 ladies who were brutally raped … sleep better tonight. He isn't coming through the window. He's in jail, and he's history."

Also present were the now-retired Paul Holes, FBI agents and others who played a role in the epic journey to bring DeAngelo to justice.

The authorities weren't done with Joseph James DeAngelo Jr.

On 25 April 2018, Orange County District Attorney Tony Rackauckas charged DeAngelo with four counts of murder. The slayings of Keith and Patrice Harrington, murdered in August 1980, would include the special circumstances of multiple murders, robbery, rape, and lying in wait. Another ticket to death row.

The Orange County complaint also covered the 6 February 1981 murder of Manuela Witthuhn, which also carried the special circumstances lever for rape, multiple murder, robbery, burglary, and lying in wait. The fourth case that the complaint covered was the Janelle Cruz homicide, which was on or about 5 May 1986. Special circumstances include rape, multiple murders, sodomy, and lying in wait.

Aside from his mugshot, the public got its first full glimpse of the California bogeyman on 27 April 2018.

If onlookers were expecting a hulking menace, they were going to be disappointed. Joseph DeAngelo appeared in a Sacramento County courtroom before Judge Michael Sweet for his arraignment hearing. DeAngelo was handcuffed to a wheelchair and appeared weak or perhaps sedated. The accused killer's answers to Judge Sweet's questions were barely audible. DeAngelo's head often slipped to the side like a curious dog or as if he were having a hard time holding it up.

Those in attendance noted that the defendant was breathing very deeply.

When asked his name, the judge had to ask DeAngelo to repeat it. And the accused said he had a lawyer – public defender Diane Howard had been appointed to represent DeAngelo.

In addition, the district attorney asked to take photos of the accused's genitals to determine if there was a "physical abnormality". Many victims had described such an abnormality, and the DA wanted confirmation.

On 10 May 2018, Santa Barbara District Attorney Joyce Dudley announced that she was charging DeAngelo with first-degree murder in the brutal slayings of Robert Offerman, Debra Alexandria Manning, Cheri Domingo and Gregory Sanchez. Special circumstances included rape, burglary and use of a firearm.

Offerman and Manning were murdered in the pre-dawn hours of 30 December 1979 by a phantom who wielded a firearm. Identical shoe prints and ligatures found at the scene tied this crime to an attempted home-invasion rape that had taken place nearby on 1 October 1979.

The evidence was eerily similar to the sexual assault rampage of the East Area Rapist in the Sacramento area. DNA tied the rapes to the murders in Santa Barbara. However, no DNA was found at the scene of the Offerman–Manning homicides. Detectives did not believe Manning was raped.

But because of the killer's actions at the crime scene, special circumstances were again tagged onto the murder charges.

DeAngelo was also indicted in the 1981 double murder of Greg Sanchez and Cheri Domingo. Sanchez was shot, suffering a non-fatal wound, while attempting to confront the intruder. Domingo was bound, and both victims were bludgeoned to death. The offender ejaculated at the crime scene, though it's not believed that Domingo was raped. Cops found the DNA evidence on a bedspread in 2011.

On 13 August 2018, the Tulare County Sheriff's Office held a press conference announcing that they would be charging DeAngelo in the 11 September 1975 murder of journalism professor Claude Snelling. He would go into the books as DeAngelo's first murder.

Snelling was shot to death while stopping a masked intruder from kidnapping his daughter. Ballistic evidence from the bullets used to shoot Snelling was matched to a gun stolen by the Visalia Ransacker in late August 1975. That made 13 charges of murder.

At the time of Snelling's murder, DeAngelo was in the embryonic stage of his criminal career, and his guise was the Visalia Ransacker. In Visalia, the defendant also fired at a police officer chasing him.

Cops explained that while there was no DNA evidence in the case, there was other physical evidence, witnesses and the Visalia Ransacker's modus operandi.

The pandemic that struck the planet in 2020 caused a number of delays in putting DeAngelo into the box. In the interim, the defence asked that the non-Sacramento County cases be tried elsewhere, calling the all-in-one approach "unconstitutional".

But among the flurry of paperwork, a *Los Angeles Times* reporter caught a footnote on a page as part of the 40-page summation on why the slayings outside Sacramento should not be tried there.

DeAngelo might be willing to plead guilty to a wide array of charges on one condition: that the death penalty be taken off the table. Media began reporting that victims and survivors had received a letter from DeAngelo's legal team offering a chance to let their feelings be known about a potential guilty plea through a third-party intermediary.

Already, four of the five district attorney offices had informed DeAngelo that should he be convicted of the homicide charges and their special circumstances, they would be seeking the death penalty against him.

But even if DeAngelo was sentenced to die, it may have been a moot point. California had recently issued a moratorium on executions. Even before the moratorium, the state had already ceased executions. Death penalty juries could also be extremely volatile and unpredictable.

The last execution occurred on 17 January 2006, when multiple killer Clarence Ray Allen caught the night train to Nowheresville at San Quentin. While no one had been executed since, there were hundreds under sentence of death, and some counties kept employing the penalty minus the execution.

In May 2020, preliminary hearings in the case were scheduled to begin. There would be more than 200 witnesses testifying over several weeks. The judge would then determine whether the evidence was a green light for a full trial on 13 murders and the 13 kidnappings/robberies that DeAngelo was charged with.

At a court appearance in January 2020, DeAngelo looked thinner and more frail with an estimated weight of around 135 pounds (61 kg). When he was busted, his weight was pegged at 205 pounds (93 kg).

While many of the sexual assaults blew past the statute of limitations, instead, DeAngelo was hit with 13 counts of kidnapping with intent to rob.

The first was as the East Area Rapist on 4 September 1976. A 29-year-old was doing her laundry alone at her parents' house when the EAR punched her, broke her nose, dragged her into the house and sexually assaulted her. He stole her car and abandoned it less than a mile from the scene.

The various district attorneys involved in the case announced they agreed on where the trial should be held. Sacramento District Attorney Anne Marie Schubert told *The Sacramento Bee*, "It began in Sacramento, and it should end in Sacramento."

Besides the symbolic reasons, the DAs argued that the trial should be held in the state capital because there were other, more practical reasons for Sacramento being the location. Convenience for witnesses, law enforcement and the trial's complexity topped the list.

Ventura County DA Gregory Totten noted the "generational impact" of the case. He said pooling of charges and resources into Sacramento shows that the prosecutors are "unified" and that it serves the case and serves justice in the best possible way. All the district attorneys wanted the case to go to trial as soon as possible, declaring victims, their survivors and the public "needs this to end".

The prosecutors added that they were looking at additional unsolved cases that could be tied to DeAngelo, but so far none had emerged.

Totten added that 10 of the 13 murder cases were death penalty eligible. That decision would be made in the future.

Schubert suggested that DeAngelo himself could speed the process up by entering a plea.

And in a move that shocked no one with familiarity with the investigation and legal process, on 29 June 2020, Joseph James DeAngelo Jr pleaded guilty at the Sacramento State University Union Ballroom. The venue was chosen as the best location for social distancing during the pandemic.

He wore an orange prison jumpsuit and appeared frail.

Prosecutors from the counties where DeAngelo had raped and murdered read out the specifics of each of his offences. Horrific detail after horrific detail ensued. The binding, the terrorizing, the robbing, the raping, the sodomizing, the beating and the killing of the innocent.

It was the small details that were the most chilling. After killing Offerman and Manning on 30 December 1979, DeAngelo sat down and snacked on leftover Christmas turkey, then scattered the bones on the patio.

"The [surviving] victims in this case have lived far too long with this trauma. They've suffered for far too many years," Ventura County District Attorney Greg Totten said. "Simply put, they deserve to see the defendant die in prison as a convict, and not simply the accused."

DeAngelo pleaded guilty to 13 counts of first-degree murder and special circumstances (including murder committed during burglaries and rapes), as well as 13 counts of kidnapping. He was not charged with any of the more than 50 rapes he committed between 1975 and 1986 because the statute of limitations had lapsed.

He answered "Guilty" 26 times during the proceedings. And he also copped to the rapes and myriad other crimes during his decade-long descent into madness by quietly saying, "I admit."

More details emerged.

Once he used fabric torn from clothes to bind a three-year-old boy while he raped the lad's mother. On another occasion, he raped a woman while her daughter was in the house.

DeAngelo agreed to plead guilty to all charges to avoid the death penalty, Sacramento County Deputy District Attorney Amy Holliday told reporters. In exchange for taking the death penalty off the table, DeAngelo will serve 11 consecutive terms of life without parole, with 15 concurrent life sentences and additional time for weapons charges, according to Holliday. He also waived his rights to appeal.

The man who gained infamy as the Golden State Killer confirmed to Superior Court Judge Michael Bowman he understood the plea deal. DeAngelo confirmed he made the plea deals of his own volition.

His arrest and guilty pleas had been a long journey for detectives up and down the state. Retired detective Larry Crompton said the rapist and killer's patterns emerged early.

"Over the years, we heard of homicides down in Southern California, and we thought it was the East Area Rapist," said Crompton, formerly of the Contra Costa County Sheriff's Department. "But he would not leave fingerprints, so we could not prove, other than his (modus operandi), that he was the same person. We did not know anything about DNA."

Thankfully, the genetic genealogist who helped catch DeAngelo did know a few things about not just DNA but also genealogy and family trees.

"To me, it was really wonderful that we're taking him from being just a suspect sitting in jail to a convicted killer and rapist because up until that point, he could have died in prison," Barbara Rae-Venter told Oxygen.com. "We got the right ending."

She said the conviction was "fabulous". Hearing the minute details of DeAngelo's horrific crimes brought the monstrosity into the sunlight, and that she later noted was difficult.

"Sitting there, listening hour after hour to the details of this sadistic, just grotesque behaviour, I'll tell you, I can't imagine what it was like for the victims. Just for me, it was really emotionally exhausting," she said.

At that point in 2020, when DeAngelo was convicted, she estimated that investigative genetic genealogy had helped solve more than 200 cold cases. Rae-Venter herself had helped close more than 30 unsolved investigations.

"I think the really big thing is that in almost all the cases, at least those that I have worked on, the person that we end up identifying was never on anybody's radar," she said, adding neither was DeAngelo. "They were somebody that, without any investigative genetic genealogy, they would have completely gotten away with it."

The final chapter in the Golden State Killer case was about to be written. His victims and survivors would finally be allowed to voice the torment and terror they had endured for decades.

When the victim impact statements from a multitude of people were read in court, it would be the coda on decades of fear.

18

Final Statements

On 21 August 2020, it was cloudy in Sacramento. The overcast skies could be partly attributed to wildfires nearby, giving the area a smoky tinge. But by the afternoon, temperatures had soared into the low nineties.

The thermometer in the Sacramento State University Union Ballroom read comfortable; figuratively, the temperature was past boiling. Scores of cops, victims, survivors, lawyers, the media and curious onlookers packed the room.

All were present to see the denouement of Joseph James DeAngelo Jr. A little more than two years earlier, the burly Vietnam vet had been arrested and charged with 13 counts of murder and 13 counts of kidnapping/robbery.

To save his life, the 75-year-old former police officer pleaded guilty on 29 June 2020, escaping a date with the death penalty. He also admitted to more than 50 rapes, although he could not be charged because of the statute of limitations in California.

Now, he was in court to learn his fate. While there would be no lethal injection, DeAngelo's remaining years would be spent in a tiny prison cell. There was no way around this. It was a case where the living might envy the dead.

And for the first time in decades, DeAngelo would be forced to hear from his victims or their proxies.

DeAngelo and the defence team – Joseph Cress, Alice Michel and Diane Howard – were seated to face Judge Michael Bowman rather than the people in attendance. The judge had made the request that he should face DeAngelo and speak with him directly.

Representing the people were Anne Marie Schubert (DA of Sacramento County); Greg Totten (DA of Ventura County); Todd Spitzer (DA of Orange County); Diana Becton (DA of Contra Costa County); Joyce Dudley (DA of Santa Barbara County); Tim Ward (DA of Tulare County); Nancy O'Malley (DA of Alameda County); and Tori Verber Salazar (DA of San Joaquin County).

DeAngelo was hammered with the maximum penalty allowed (notwithstanding the death penalty) by law. He was sentenced to 11 consecutive life sentences without the possibility of parole. Dozens more years were added for the special enhancements and additional charges.

When everyone was seated, Judge Bowman began the grim task of reading the 26 charges that the Golden State Killer had pleaded guilty to. He also read into the record DeAngelo's other admissions of burglary and rape. These crimes were to be factored into the judge's sentencing.

For decades, the victims had essentially been voiceless, with only a handful of prosecutors and cops as their advocates. The heinous crimes inflicted on their families lost to the passage of time. But now it was their time.

DeAngelo did not look at them; instead, he sat stone-faced, appearing indifferent to the terrible suffering he had inflicted on his victims' families. He stared silently at a wall.

And then, one by one, family and friends of the 13 people the Golden State Killer had senselessly butchered unburdened their troubled souls and delivered their anguished truth.

First to speak was Elizabeth Hupp, whose father, Claude Snelling, sacrificed his life for his daughter's. He was DeAngelo's first known victim in the murder stakes. Hupp's statement followed two days of victim impact statements from those he had raped and assaulted.

"What sickens me most is that DeAngelo was able to live a normal life with his family for all those years," Hupp said.

Snelling was attempting to interrupt the Visalia Ransacker from abducting his 16-year-old daughter in September 1975. The journalism professor was shot to death.

Earlier, Hupp told how she saw a man peering into her bedroom window about a month before. Now, he was in her bedroom, and he was whisking her out of the home when her dad confronted the masked man and started running towards him to rescue Elizabeth.

Her dad's killer squeezed the trigger two times, hitting her dad and killing him. He kicked Hupp in the face.

"For many years, I felt guilt for what happened that night," she said. "I thought maybe there was something I could have said or done to keep him from coming out that night. My dad was such a gentle soul and loving, kind-hearted man who loved his family more than anything. My dad saved my life that night, and he's my hero."

DeAngelo also shot Visalia police detective William McGowen, who nearly captured him several months after the Snelling murder. He survived his wounds but died in 2005. Still, the horror of that night hung over the cop's family until the end of his days.

"By the grace of God, dad was only slightly injured," Lori Mendonca said of her father. "My father felt a personal responsibility to solve the case for the Snelling family. My father never stopped looking for the Ransacker. Every person who resembled the composite he would check out.

"It never ended."

After murdering Claude Snelling and trying to kill Detective William McGowen, the Visalia Ransacker's days were numbered in the sleepy community. There were greener pastures in the eastern suburbs of Sacramento, and it was closer to DeAngelo's home and new job with the Auburn Police Department. He would now be the East Area Rapist and soon resumed his night-time prowling.

One such expedition in Rancho Cordova came off the rails in February 1978 when he encountered a young couple out for a walk. Wearing a ski mask, he chased Brian Maggiore, 22, an airman, and his wife Katie, 20. He first shot Brian, then cornered Katie in between one of the suburban bungalows. She screamed, "Help me! Help me!"

But there would be no mercy from the East Area Rapist, and he shot and killed Katie as well.

"DeAngelo chased her down and shot her in cold blood," her brother Ken Smith said in his victim impact statement as the doomed couple's wedding photos flashed on a screen behind him.

"Katie and Brian were special, and we all loved them so much. DeAngelo, you hurt our families and other families so much. But now that's over. You lurked in the dark so you could prey on innocent victims. Now you are the prey, DeAngelo. You're not important. We will remember Brian and Katie for the rest of our lives. But after you are sentenced, you are nothing."

After the Maggiore murders, the Golden State Killer again took his act on the road. San Joaquin Valley, the Central Coast, and he again dialled it back in his home turf of Sacramento. But after three murders, his bloodlust was far from sated.

On 30 December 1979, DeAngelo entered a condominium in Goleta in Santa Barbara County, pried open a sliding glass door and attacked Debra Alexandria Manning and Robert Offerman. After binding both with cord, he raped Manning and shot her in the back of her head.

DeAngelo shot Offerman three times when he slipped out of his binds.

Then, sometime between 13 March and 16 March 1980, he tied up Lyman and Charlene Smith with drapery cord at their Ventura home. He then bludgeoned the couple to death with a piece of firewood. Lyman's son, Gary, 12, found their bodies.

For his sister, Jennifer Carole, the murders turned her life upside down. She had been close with her stepmother, Charlene. She wondered aloud in court whether her father, a lawyer and former prosecutor, would have become a judge.

"My dad, a Democrat with political ambitions, would have likely been appointed to the bench, and then later he would have run for office," she said in her statement. "I have no doubt that he would have won. As a political junkie, I likely would have participated in his campaign, and who knows where that might have taken me."

But that was not to be. The murders have been a dark spectre over her entire life. She said she regretted the plea deal.

"Predictably, Joe decided to forego his manhood and take the easy way out," she said. "Interestingly, manhood is defined as having courage, strength and, ironically, sexual potency. It's not surprising that, once again, Joe's lack of manhood is the spectacle."

Jennifer Carole was also bitter that DeAngelo's family was allowed to sell his home and that he didn't spend any money on defence lawyers. Instead, public defenders were appointed to handle his case, leaving taxpayers with the tab.

"Joe took what he wanted at every turn," she said. "In collusion with his wife, he liquidated and transferred his assets. He's using a public defender. He gamed the system so he could sit here with remarkable legal representation at taxpayer expense. These are the hallmarks of white privilege."

Bruce Harrington had been at the forefront of the campaign to secure DNA samples from felons into the hands of law enforcement. His brother and his wife, Keith and Patrice Harrington, were bludgeoned to death at their Dana Point home in Orange County in August 1980. The killer had raped Patrice.

Bruce and his brother Ron appeared before the judge together.

"Have you thought about the many lives that have been affected?" Ron Harrington asked, glaring at DeAngelo.

"Have you thought about how many lives were changed because of that? Remember some of the rape victims were just 13 and 15 years old. The Golden State Killer truly is the worst of the worst, 13 murders, 50 rapes. He is the most prolific murder rapist ever. His crimes were so brutal, so heinous, so sadistic. He is just a violent sexual predator. Pure evil."

He added, "Seven weeks ago, on June 29, I was before your honour. I was in the courtroom when all the pleas were taken. I listened to all those guilty pleas. I listened to all those admissions of all those rape cases and related crimes. He appeared weak and feeble. It was just a facade. I listened as the prosecutors described virtually identical offences over and over again like a broken record. As the afternoon wore on, I was getting physically sick. I just kept thinking, there can't be any more crimes. They continued all afternoon. At the end of the day, there were 161 separate crimes."

David Witthuhn would not live to see justice for his wife, Manuela, or for himself. Manuela was raped and murdered by the Golden State Killer in February 1981. But for years, a cloud of suspicion hovered over her husband, and it took until 1997 to clear his name. By then, it was too late. He was a wreck and died in 2008.

Manuela's brother-in-law, Drew Witthuhn, during his victim impact statement, described DeAngelo as "this convict" or "it", and likened his guilty plea to a war crimes tribunal for the number of "casualties" he inflicted.

Witthuhn was a cop for twenty years.

"And for this convict's edification, a real one. Your honour, this thing was no cop," he said. "Manuela was nothing more to this convict than one more kill, one more trophy, one more body."

For decades, Debbi Domingo McMullan had been plagued with questions about the night her mother died and the man who murdered her and her boyfriend at the home where she was staying in Goleta in Santa Barbara County.

DeAngelo found Cheri Domingo and Greg Sanchez in bed in July 1981. He shot Sanchez in the face and then bludgeoned him an estimated 24 times. He tied up Cheri Domingo, then raped her before bludgeoning her to death.

When she approached the lectern in the makeshift courthouse, Debbi Domingo McMullan glared at DeAngelo.

"Did she beg for her life?" McMullan said to DeAngelo. "Did the monster say anything to her? Did he reveal his face before smashing hers?"

She then wiped the tears streaming down her face. "I'm sorry, I can't see through my tears," she said.

Her mom and Sanchez were a happy couple who loved to dance. But after they were murdered, McMullan's life spiralled down the drain. There were the drugs, she said. She lost her kids to Child Protective Services, hit bottom, then found salvation as a devout Christian. She now ministers to convicts in Texas prisons.

McMullan took ownership of her own mistakes and didn't blame the killer for them. She told the court she took comfort knowing the bleak future of the man who murdered her mother.

"[He must be] nervous as hell because everyone in prison will know exactly who he is and what deplorable things he has done," she said. "Tonight, DeAngelo will toss and turn on that cold, steel bunk in his cell, knowing the trauma he caused to hundreds, including his own family."

She added, "He will spend eternity alone wishing he had lived his life differently. Tonight, I will sleep soundly and in my dreams see my mom and Greg smiling, still dancing."

After the Domingo–Sanchez murders, the killer seemed to go into a deep slumber, nearly five years without a peep. But he was poised for one last hurrah. Janelle Cruz, 18 years old, would be his comeback and coda.

Then, out of the blue, he struck. On 5 May 1986, he broke into the Cruz home in Irvine, tied up, raped and bludgeoned Janelle to death.

Janelle's sister Michelle said in her victim impact statement that DeAngelo was a "cruel, pathetic piece of scum". She noted that in the wake of Janelle's murder, her killer was able to carry on, leading his life. Janelle was not able to do that. She added that her sister had been beaten so badly, the family had to have a closed casket.

"He basically had a good, full life," Michelle Cruz said. "On the other hand, I will never be an aunt, my kids will never have cousins, my mom will never see her daughter go to college or get married.

"No normal person can do what he did to Janelle, and I feel sorry for his soul," she said.

Then it was the turn of the gathered district attorneys at the podium.

Orange County DA Todd Spitzer told the court it was remarkable how DeAngelo was able to obliterate so many lives over so many years but yet was able to live his own life. He was able to "be on his boat" and "blow out birthday candles with his family".

Tulare County DA Tim Ward said the Golden State Killer investigation should give some hope to victims and their families in other cold cases. "Now they know to never give up. The space for evil like this to operate grows smaller and smaller."

He added that the "true legacy" of the Golden State Killer case is the hope it gave victims of other crimes.

Anne Marie Schubert, DA for Sacramento County, said for those affected by the Golden State Killer and the community at large, the greatest revenge against DeAngelo is for the victims to live their lives. Schubert said, "Paint your children and your grandchildren's rooms again with hearts and rainbows. Water ski again."

And she also aimed at the killer before her.

"There is honestly little left to say. Your name will fade from the headlines," she said, adding that he would never be able to "manipulate" or "deceive" state corrections into believing he is a feeble old man who deserves a break. This statement triggered thunderous applause from the gallery.

And she quoted Kris Pedretti who had been raped by DeAngelo when she was a teenager. "Mr DeAngelo, there is no prayer strong enough to save you," she said to renewed applause.

Defence lawyer Alice Michel acknowledged the victims and had heard their dark truths. She said she hoped that DeAngelo's confession offered some measure of peace for the survivors.

Shockingly, family members and a friend of DeAngelo had brief statements read in the court. But his lawyers were emphatic that the statements were not justifications for his twisted actions or to trigger more pain in the victims. And the defence team pleaded for the media and the public to give them privacy.

"They are innocent," one defence lawyer said.

His sister wrote in her statement that DeAngelo and his siblings had endured cruel "mental and physical" abuse at the hands of their father early in their lives. "Joe faced many things and I'm sure he couldn't cope with it all. It will never justify what happened," his sister wrote, adding her "deepest sympathy to all victims and survivors".

A niece said DeAngelo was like a father to her, while a friend related how close he had been with his family and repeated his difficult early years. Another niece also expressed sympathy to the victims and their families. She painted a portrait of normalcy.

But she added: "There is someone else inside of him who I do not know. I'm very sorry to the victims. I can't imagine what they went through."

Now, it was Joseph James DeAngelo's opportunity to speak. He emerged, standing from his wheelchair. He did not appear infirm or ailing in any way on that hot day in August.

DeAngelo then faced the judge, pausing only to remove his COVID-19 mask. Court observers said there were nuances in his movements. What they meant, no one was sure. Gone was the feeble, elderly man's voice. He spoke clearly and strongly.

"I've listened to all of your statements. Each one of 'em. And I'm truly sorry to everyone I've hurt. Thank you, your honour," he said, then sat down.

Judge Bowman thanked DeAngelo and then moved to the imposition of sentence. There had been much to consider, including the victim impact statements, the sordid facts and the circumstances of the wide-ranging investigation. The jurist also officially approved the plea bargain that removed the death penalty from the equation.

Bowman said he accepted the plea bargain for the defendant, who had been facing the death penalty, because Governor

Gavin Newsom had put a moratorium on capital punishment in the state. The judge said the deal spared victims' survivors the "unimaginable emotions by sitting through such a trial", and "finally, taxpayers save tens of millions of dollars".

Bowman added he was "not saying Mr DeAngelo does not deserve to have the death penalty imposed", but "it will never come to pass".

And Judge Bowman cited the multitude of victim impact statements that laid bare decades of violence and cruelty, a catalogue of what-ifs and could-have-beens if those lives had not been snuffed out.

"Their impact statements will always be with me. I was moved by their grace … qualities you clearly lack," he said, addressing DeAngelo. Judge Bowman noted that during the court proceedings, he wondered whether the serial killer was "comprehending the anguish" he had caused.

That question may never be answered. Because there was no trial and no pre-sentencing report, we only know snippets of the life of Joseph James DeAngelo Jr. His childhood is only instructive to a point. Therefore, the world may never know what demonic forces made him a monster.

One thing was certain: he would never again see the light of day. He was sentenced to 11 consecutive sentences of life without the possibility of parole. Judge Bowman added years to his sentence with enhancements for murder during the commission of rape, murder during the commission of burglary, and for the use of weapons during the commission of these crimes.

DeAngelo, 80 at the time of writing, will only emerge from prison in a pine box.

He was also ordered to pay $10,000 in restitution to the family of Janelle Cruz. The Irvine teen's murder was the only one covered by the enforceable civil judgment because the relevant laws were not in place until 1985, the year before her death.

In addition, DeAngelo was ordered to register as a sex offender (albeit a moot point), submit to an AIDS test, provide thumb and palm prints, provide DNA, and not possess firearms (again, moot). Under the plea deal, the serial murderer has no right to appeal his sentence.

As the court was adjourned, and DeAngelo taken away to begin the grim new life he deserves, the gallery broke into applause.

Outside the temporary courthouse, the prosecutors held a press conference where one by one, they discussed the blockbuster case.

Todd Spitzer, DA of Orange County, was the most vehement, slamming DeAngelo's apology as "fake" and a "sham", and the resolution of the four-decade-old case as "one of the proudest moments" in his career as a prosecutor.

"Mr DeAngelo tried to pull a fast one on all of us," Spitzer said. "Who did he leave out? The people who say they love him. He didn't just destroy your lives. Can you imagine being the daughter of Joseph DeAngelo, going through life asking yourself if he passed on his genetic framework? ... The same for his former wife, the betrayal of their marriage ... It was a sham. It was not remorseful. He failed to apologize to important people."

Before sentencing, the Orange County DA issued a statement recalling that when he was elected, he said he wanted to make it a priority to seek the death penalty for DeAngelo.

Spitzer said he had hoped to see the Golden State Killer strapped to a gurney and headed for a lethal injection in the green room at San Quentin "and watch you silently slip into the night ... never again to take away anyone's dreams you ruined or the nightmares you created ... You made it personal, and it was personal for me. I believe this person – not even a person, this beast – deserved the ultimate punishment of death."

But Spitzer conceded that given the historical nature of the case, the plea deal was the "right thing to do".

Ventura County District Attorney Greg Totten noted that it was a "case about light and darkness", and the victim impact statements "shined a very bright light on the magnitude of the crimes before this court and painted a picture of the immense impact these horrific crimes had on their lives".

And with that, the press conference concluded.

Retired investigator Paul Holes said in 2021 that the case took a terrible toll on his life, including PTSD and a shattered marriage. He lived and breathed the Golden State Killer and his precursors for 24 years. While DeAngelo has been identified and convicted, sometimes, that's not enough.

Holes said that while the victims and their families "got an answer", it still "has not provided any relief from the trauma that they have suffered for decades".

"It is still a healing process for them, and many of them will probably never totally recover," Holes explained to *E! News*. "And it just speaks to the gravity of the crimes that he did."

Now retired, Holes has become a rock star in the world of true crime, with a podcast and a TV show, and is in high demand for speaking engagements.

Those involved in the case believe if not for DNA technology and the pioneering use of genetic genealogy, it is unlikely DeAngelo would have been caught.

"If it wasn't for that DNA, his name would never have surfaced – period," Schubert told *People*. "There was a needle in that haystack, and we found that damn needle."

In November 2020, Joseph DeAngelo was transferred to the North Kern State Prison near Bakersfield. As of February 2025, the Golden State Killer is incarcerated in protective custody at

California State Prison, Corcoran, about 40 minutes south of Visalia.

At various times, the prison has held some of the country's most notorious serial killers and other well-known murderers, including the Dating Game Killer, Rodney Alcala, and cult leader Charles Manson.

Today, Joseph James DeAngelo Jr is the prison's best-known convict.

Bibliography

ABC7 News. 4 May 2018. *'Golden State Killer' suspect once planned to kill ex-police chief who fired him.* https://abc7news.com/golden-state-killer-arrested-east-area-rapist-visalia-ransacker-joseph-james-deangelo/3423964/

Aradillas, Elaine. 9 May 2018. People. *Golden State Killer Suspect Was 'Grouchy Old Man,' Says Restaurant Owner Who Often Waited on Him.* https://people.com/crime/golden-state-killer-joseph-deangelo-angry-restaurant-customer/

Baer, Stephanie K. 14 May 2018. BuzzFeed News. *The Suspected Golden State Killer Witnessed Two Men Rape His Sister. It May Have Fueled His Rampage.* https://www.buzzfeednews.com/article/skbaer/the-suspected-golden-state-killer-witnessed-two-men-rape

Bizjak, Tony; Chabria, Anita; Kasler, Dale; Chavez, Nashelly; and Lambert, Diana. 26 April 2018. The Sacramento Bee. *He was quirky and complex. But they never thought the former cop next door could be notorious.* https://www.sacbee.com/latest-news/article209792989.html

Brinkley, Leslie. 2 May 2018. ABC7 News. *Walnut Creek 'Golden State Killer' victim describes details of attack, hope for future.* https://

abc7news.com/golden-state-killer-arrested-east-area-rapist-visalia-ransacker-joseph-james-deangelo/3415465/

Cary, Nathaniel. 6 November 2016. Greenville News. *Chilling Amazon product reviews catch attention of Kohlhepp investigators*. https://www.greenvilleonline.com/story/news/crime/2016/11/06/chilling-amazon-product-reviews-catch-attention-kohlhepp-investigators/93403782/

City News Service. 21 August 2020. ABC 10NEWS. *Golden State Killer Joseph DeAngelo sentenced to life in prison without parole*. https://www.10news.com/news/golden-state-killer-joseph-deangelo-to-be-sentenced

Cummings, Brandi. 1 June 2018. KCRA 3. *Q&A: Daughter whose loss helped break the East Area Rapist case*. https://www.kcra.com/article/qanda-daughter-whose-loss-helped-break-the-east-area-rapist-case/21006357

Danielsen, Shelby. 12 May 2018. First Coast News. *Jacksonville Mother of last known murder victim of the Golden State Killer breaks her silence*. https://www.firstcoastnews.com/article/news/exclusive-mother-of-last-known-murder-victim-of-the-golden-state-killer-breaks-her-silence/77-551490360

Deutsch, Linda and Thompson, Don. 8 June 2013. The Associated Press. *Calif. serial killer Richard Ramirez dies*. https://apnews.com/general-news-d4e75396582d4da19cd3623d27e13b22

Dillon, Nancy. 25 May 2018. New York Daily News. *What Golden State Killer suspect Joseph DeAngelo has been doing all these years*. https://www.nydailynews.com/2018/04/26/what-golden-state-killer-suspect-joseph-deangelo-has-been-doing-all-these-years/

Domingo, Debbi and Minutaglio, Rose. 25 April 2018. Good Housekeeping. *The Golden State Killer Brutally Murdered My Mother.* https://www.goodhousekeeping.com/life/a19515171/golden-state-killer-survivor-interview/

Douglass, Joe. 28 April 2018. KATU. *'What did I miss?': Retired 'Golden State Killer' investigator in Oregon reacts to arrest.* https://katu.com/news/local/what-did-i-miss-retired-golden-state-killer-investigator-in-oregon-reacts-to-arrest

Dowd, Katie. 28 November 2021. SFGATE. *A California oil heiress was strangled in her apartment. Who got away with murder?* https://www.sfgate.com/unsolved/article/California-oil-heiress-strangled-in-home-16632427.php

Effron, Lauren; Halaban, Boaz; and Dorian, Marc. 19 March 2020. *How a Jane Doe child case uncovered a serial killer, identified victims and changed the use of DNA forensics.* https://abcnews.go.com/US/jane-doe-child-case-uncovered-serial-killer-identified/story?id=69648434

Federal Bureau of Investigation. 15 June 2016. *Cold Case Killer: Help Us Catch the East Area Rapist.* https://www.fbi.gov/news/stories/help-us-catch-the-east-area-rapist

Federal Bureau of Investigation. 15 June 2016. *FBI Announces $50,000 Reward and National Campaign to Identify East Area Rapist/Golden State Killer.* https://www.fbi.gov/contact-us/field-offices/sacramento/news/press-releases/fbi-announces-50-000-reward-and-national-campaign-to-identify-east-area-rapist-golden-state-killer

Gilbertson, Annie. 26 April 2018. LAist. *Until DNA tied his wife's murder to serial killer, an OC man under suspicion 'went off the deep end'.* https://laist.com/news/kpcc-archive/before-nabbing-alleged-golden-state-killer-police

Gros, Chris. 21 August 2020. CBS8. *Golden State Killer sentenced to life in prison without possibility of parole.* https://www.cbs8.com/article/news/crime/golden-state-killer-sentencing/509-505138e6-d899-495a-a936-dc29433e920e

Hicks, Jerry. 23 August 1980. Los Angeles Times. *Young Couple Murdered in Niguel Shores*

Hutchinson, Bill. 3 May 2018. ABC News. *Why 'Golden State Killer' may have stopped murder spree: Investigator Paul Holes, a retired detective, investigated the case for decades.* https://abcnews.go.com/US/golden-state-killer-stopped-murder-spree-investigator/story?id=54906116

Hunter, Brad. 8 May 2018. Toronto Sun. *Golden State Killer tormented victim's hubby for decades.* https://torontosun.com/news/world/golden-state-killer-tormented-victims-hubby-for-decades

Hunter, Brad. 22 November 2021. Toronto Sun. *HUNTER: How Los Angeles cops caught army of 1970's serial killers.* https://torontosun.com/news/world/hunter-how-los-angeles-cops-caught-army-of-1970s-serial-killers

Hunter, Brad. 8 December 2022. Toronto Sun. *HUNTER: Joseph Augustus Zarelli named as Boy in the Box murder victim.* https://torontosun.com/news/world/hunter-joseph-augustus-zarelli-named-as-boy-in-the-box-murder-victim

ISHI News. 7 May 2019. *To Catch a Predator – An Interview with Paul Holes.* https://www.ishinews.com/to-catch-a-predator-an-interview-with-paul-holes/

ISHI News. 5 Dec 2019. *Identifying the Golden State Killer: An Interview with Paul Holes and Barbara Rae-Venter.* https://www.youtube.com/watch?v=ecwzHDVdXvw&t=85s&ab_channel=ISHINews

Kelly, Peggy. 13 October 2000. Santa Paula Times. *Lyman & Charlene Smith murder revealed to be work of serial killer.* https://santapaulatimes.com/news/archivestory.php/aid/1627/Lyman___Charlene_Smith_murder_revealed_to_be_work_of_serial_killer.html

Kenton, Luke. 30 January 2022. The Sun. *DRACULA KILLER: I found my pregnant wife's disemboweled body after 'Vampire of Sacramento' serial killer cut her up and drank her blood.* https://

www.the-sun.com/news/4563217/vampire-sacramento-killer-victim-speaks-pregnant-wife-murder/

Kiger, Patrick J. 28 May 2025. HISTORY. *How the Dust Bowl Made Americans Refugees in Their Own Country.* https://www.history.com/articles/dust-bowl-migrants-california

Lusher, Adam. 26 April 2018. Independent. *Who is the Golden State Killer? How an ex-cop is suspected of inflicting a reign of terror on California.* https://www.independent.co.uk/news/world/americas/golden-state-killer-joseph-james-deangelo-latest-california-east-area-rapist-crimes-cop-life-story-what-he-did-a8323976.html

McFall, Marni Rose. 9 October 2024. Newsweek. *Map Shows States With The Most Recorded Serial Killers.* https://www.newsweek.com/map-shows-states-most-serial-killers-1966333

McNamara, Michelle. 27 February 2013. Los Angeles magazine. *In The Footsteps of a Killer: The Writer's Cut.* https://lamag.com/news/in-the-footsteps-of-a-killer-the-writers-cut

Murphy, Jessica. 31 August 2018. BBC News. *Why were there so many serial killers in the 1980s?* https://www.bbc.com/news/world-us-canada-45324622

Novak, Sara. 9 October 2023. Discover. *Why Do Serial Killers Take Breaks, and Do They Ever Stop Killing?* https://www.discovermagazine.com/the-sciences/why-do-serial-killers-take-breaks-and-do-they-ever-stop-killing

NPR. 10 August 2022. *After a career of cracking cold cases, investigator Paul Holes opens up.* https://www.npr.org/transcripts/1116304728

Parvini, Sarah; Mozingo, Joe; Winton, Richard; and Serna, Joseph. 27 April 2018. Los Angeles Times. *Quiet life, with flashes of rage: Golden State Killer suspect is recalled as a 'cantankerous' neighbor with a bad temper.* https://enewspaper.latimes.com/infinity/article_share.aspx?guid=b0091003-c279-48f8-afd7-c1e7f0099eab

Pedretti, Kris. 22 June 2021. SBS News. *Golden State Killer: woman reveals path to healing after surviving attack from serial killer.* https://www.sbs.com.au/news/insight/article/golden-state-killer-woman-reveals-path-to-healing-after-surviving-attack-from-serial-killer/1ao5641ff

Ray, Alyssa. 24 April 2021. E! News. *Paul Holes Reflects on the Golden State Killer Case 3 Years After Joseph James DeAngelo Jr.'s Arrest.* https://www.eonline.com/news/1262161/paul-holes-reflects-on-the-golden-state-killer-case-3-years-after-joseph-james-deangelo-jr-s-arrest

Sederstrom, Jill. 1 July 2020. Oxygen. *'We Got The Right Ending': Genetic Genealogist Who Helped Put Golden State Killer Away Reflects On His Guilty Plea.* https://www.oxygen.com/crime-news/barbara-rae-vente-reacts-to-golden-state-killer-joseph-deangelos-guilty-plea

Serna, Joseph. 8 June 2018. Los Angeles Times. *Wife of Golden State Killer suspect offers prayers for victims, seeks privacy for family.* https://www.latimes.com/local/lanow/la-me-golden-state-killer-wife-20180608-story.html

Serna, Joseph and Oreskes, Benjamin. 25 May 2018. Los Angeles Times. *Must Reads: Why did it take so long to arrest the Golden State Killer suspect? Interagency rivalries, old technology, errors and bad luck.* https://www.latimes.com/local/lanow/la-me-ln-golden-state-killer-case-20180525-story.html

Shapiro, Emily; Johnson, Whit; and Harrison, Jenna. 26 April 2018. The Sacramento Bee. *Suspected 'Golden State Killer' seemed shocked by arrest, told police he had a roast in the oven: Official.* https://abcnews.go.com/US/suspected-golden-state-killer-shocked-arrest-told-police/story?id=54746113

Simon, Neal. 1 July 2018. The Evening Tribune. *Looking for DeAngelo's Bath story.* https://www.eveningtribune.com/story/news/crime/2018/07/01/looking-for-deangelo-s-bath/11620814007/

Stewart, Sara. 14 February 2019. New York Post. *Why this family is convinced its patriarch is the Black Dahlia killer.* https://nypost.com/2019/02/13/why-this-family-is-convinced-its-patriarch-is-the-black-dahlia-killer

Stanton, Sam and Lillis, Ryan. 27 April 2018. The Sacramento Bee. *Relative's DNA from genealogy websites cracked East Area Rapist case, DA's office says.* https://www.sacbee.com/latest-news/article209913514.html

Stanton, Sam. 15 March 2019. The Sacramento Bee. *Exclusive: Sacramento cops arrested Golden State Killer suspect in 1996, then let him go.* https://www.sacbee.com/news/california/article227901874.html

Stanton, Sam and Smith, Darrell. 21 August 2020. The Sacramento Bee. *'You are nothing:' Relatives of Golden State Killer's murder victims confront DeAngelo.* https://www.sacbee.com/news/local/article245088385.html

St John, Paige. Los Angeles Times. *Man in the Window.* https://www.latimes.com/projects/man-in-the-window-joe-DeAngelo-golden-state-killer-serial/

The Atlantic. *Chasing a Ghost.* https://www.theatlantic.com/sponsored/hbo-gone-dark/Chasing-a-Ghost/3415

Tron, Gina. 9 May 2018. Oxygen. *Why Did the Golden State Killer Stop Killing?* https://www.oxygen.com/crime-time/why-did-the-golden-state-killer-stop-killing

Wolf, Ali. 18 February 2019. Fox40. *Joseph DeAngelo's Pending Divorce Could Impact East Area Rapist Trial.* https://fox40.com/news/local-news/joseph-deangelos-pending-divorce-could-impact-east-area-rapist-trial/